ROAD TO THE FINAL HOUR

THE CATASTROPHIC TAX CONSEQUENCES OF THE PROFESSIONALIZATION OF COLLEGE SPORTS

THOMAS A. McGOVERN, CPA

Dedication

This book is dedicated to
Thomas P. McGovern

Contents

Prologue

Given the recent developments in intercollegiate sports, it is important for action to be taken now at the national level to avoid further descent into commercialization and ultimately professionalization. Herein it is argued for a nonprofessional system that allows student athletes to benefit financially while preserving the favorable tax status of the industry.

With the government refocusing on national priorities following the election cycle, it is an opportune time to highlight the issues facing an institution that is endearing to a significant number of Americans. While other concerns will likely take precedent in the near term, these trends will need to be addressed in the next couple of years lest we proceed inexorably down a path that is certain to produce adverse results.

Introduction

On May 23, 2024, the National Collegiate Athletic Association (NCAA) announced a milestone settlement of a number of pending antitrust suits. The NCAA agreed to pay $2.75 billion in damages to former college athletes who were deprived of compensation for media rights, image, and likeness usage during the period when renumeration for these activities was proscribed by NCAA rules. In addition, the settlement outlines a revenue sharing arrangement whereby up to 22 percent of revenue will be shared with athletes, albeit the announcement was short on the details of how this would be effected.

The settlement came as a shock to many, and the sports media heralded it as the "death of amateurism." Whether panic over the ramifications of this agreement is warranted is certainly debatable. One thing for sure is that it leaves the industry in a state of uncertainty that is unprecedented in its more than a century of existence.

While less focused on by the media than the implications for Title IX, roster sizes, and recruitment, this unforeseen development does again raise the age-old question of whether revenue generated from college sporting events should be taxed. It is a conversation that has been ongoing among accounting professionals and athletics officials for decades, although it has been given sparse attention by the mainstream sports and even financial press. Nonetheless it is an increasingly important question, especially as the evolution of college sports has accelerated in just the last five years.

Historically, intercollegiate athletics has benefitted from a twofold charitable exemption in the tax code—their educational value and their amateur status. Even as amateurism decays in the wake of the recent settlement, I argue here that college sports can still avail itself of both exemptions. However, if the industry moves too far in the direction of professionalism, I argue that it risks losing them both.

My impetus for writing this tome came seven years ago at a conference for college and university governing boards. At this conference, trustees from institutions across the United States discussed the pertinent issues of the time. In 2017, these included freedom of speech on campus, declining enrollment, cost of education, financial issues, and, of course, intercollegiate athletics. It is here that I learned of the consternation among education officials at the trends in college sports. Many were concerned that a more professionalized model would not only be more costly and strip funds away from nonrevenue sports, but it would also dispossess them of the tax advantages they had enjoyed since its existence. As one put it, "we will have killed the golden goose."

It is therefore my primary objective herein to shed light on this issue and its critical relevance to an important U.S. institution. In pursuit of this objective, I think it is also important to provide some background on both the tax code as well as the history of intercollegiate competition. I expect there are two audiences for this book, which will overlap significantly. Those who are college sports fans will likely be the largest group, although certainly not mutually exclusive with the second group, who are those with a background or interest in accounting and finance. I expect both constituencies will benefit from a background on both pillars of this literary piece— college sports and tax accounting.

As a secondary objective, I provide some recommendations on conduct of policy that can avoid the catastrophic consequences of a worst-case scenario. Whether decision-makers agree with these recommendations, or are even reading this work, time will tell, but this book is primarily aimed at the public. Nonetheless, you will discover from reading further that none of my recommendations are idealist in nature but rather constitute a pragmatic strategy for navigating the challenges ahead.

In a third, but certainly not least important, objective, I am attempting to call the reader to action. We must convince decision-makers and policy deciders to take heed of the potential outcomes that everyone wants to avoid and be judicious in their course of action. While it may not be possible to reverse course given the sensitivity of the issues, it is certainly prudent to consider another path going forward to avoid exacerbating the problem.

I also want to provide a disclaimer on certain of the content in this manuscript. First, tax policy, other than what is written in the IRC, is by its nature fluid. We can look to precedent cases and decisions to infer what future guidance will look like, but there is no certainty as to the position the IRS or Treasury Department will take on a particular issue. What exists henceforth represents my best guess as a CPA and finance professional as to what we can expect in various scenarios.

Also, it is common in the tax world for accountants and attorneys to overlap significantly in their disciplines. The tax code is, after all, part of the law—U.S. Code Title 26 to be specific. In those areas that involve statutory discussion, be aware that while I have worked closely with lawyers over the years, I am not an attorney, and nothing stated should be construed as the opinion of a legal professional.

Certainly nothing in the following pages should be taken as tax advice for any individual or business. Readers should consult their tax advisor on any tax issues germane to their personal or entity finances. What is discussed here concerns tax consideration for some of the largest institutions in the country and has little applicability outside of that context.

Also, there are instances in this book that discuss the current equivalence of monetary sums stated in historical context. For calculations of the future value of monetary sums, the assumption is a simple 2% long term rate of inflation. While there certainly have been time periods, including recently, where inflation outpaced this target, it is being used here for simplicity as a long run average.

With that, I hope everyone enjoys reading this and is educated and enlightened as to the importance of this issue—and will think about taking action by telling friends and supporting the cause to preserve college sports as they are today in the United States.

1

Evolution of the Tax Code

When Benjamin Franklin stated that the only certainties in life were "death and taxes," he may not have contemplated how accurate a prediction it would become. Taxes have influenced nearly every aspect of our lives as they have the progress of history. Herein we discuss the origins of the tax code and how it has developed over the last century and a half to its current manifestation.

The origins of U.S. tax law date back to the 19th century, but it was not until the early part of the 20th century that it was codified into a centralized source.[1] In fact, federal income taxes were prohibited under the original Constitution, as they were "direct" taxes whereas the government only had the right to impose "indirect" taxes such as tariffs and excise levies. However, during the Civil War, Congress was required to find a way to generate additional revenue to support the federal military.[2]

At the start of the war, the Revenue Act of 1861 became the first attempt at a federal income tax.[2] The law imposed a 3 percent assessment on incomes of more than $800, which is the equivalent of roughly $20k today. Under the weight of extreme opposition, the Act was repealed in 1872.[2]

In 1894, the Wilson-Gorman Tariff Act was passed.[2] The legislation was advanced by farmers in the South and West, through groups such as the Greenback Party, in an attempt to lower burdensome tariffs. It established a 2 percent tax on incomes of more than $4,000, which would equate to $52,500 in 2024. Again, opposition was fierce, and the law was ultimately ruled unconstitutional by the Supreme Court.

Arguments against a federal income tax were based primarily on their classification as direct taxes. Direct taxes are paid directly to the government, and their impact cannot be mitigated by passing the cost to other parties.[2] Property taxes are a form of direct tax, whereas sales taxes are considered an indirect tax. Under the U.S. Constitution at the time, the federal government could only impose direct taxes in a manner that was proportionate to the population. As such, detractors argued that this precluded it from creating a broad-based income tax that ignored differences in state populations.

For an income tax to be compliant with the proportionate impact guideline, it would be required to be graduated in a way that imposed a higher levy on more populated states such that the per capita amount of taxation in each state was equivalent. As such, the tax in a state like New York would be required to be more costly on an aggregate basis than in a state like Alabama, as it is assumed that the former's economy and population would be strong enough to support it vis-à-vis the latter. Given such a complication, this type of progressive regime was unideal for maximum revenue generation

Additional fodder for the campaign against federal income taxes was provided by reference to the American Revolution as a renunciation of British taxation power. Historians have since highlighted that the American Revolution was fought for a myriad of reasons, many of which were unrelated to taxes. Nonetheless, this context did provide some fuel for the opposition.

The year 1909 saw the first corporate income tax with an excise charge of 1 percent on profits of more than $5,000.[2] Once again, it was wildly unpopular. The 1909 law reestablished the principal of taxing corporations separately from individuals originally included in the Revenue Act of 1894 that was deemed unconstitutional.[2] While this law itself was ultimately repealed, it is considered the flagship of the practice of corporate taxation that persists today.

In 1913, with World War I looming in Europe, Wyoming become the 36th state to ratify the 16th Amendment to the U.S. Constitution proposed by President Taft four years earlier.[2] The amendment gave the federal government taxation authority over corporate and individual incomes. Specifically, it stated: "Congress shall have the power to lay and collect taxes on incomes, from whatever source derived, without apportionment among the several states, and without regard to any census or enumeration."[2] Shortly thereafter, Congress enacted a flat tax on personal income of more than $3,000 that later morphed into a graduated income tax.

It took a Constitutional amendment to usher in the tax environment that U.S. citizens have lived with for over a hundred years. Then, as now, the concept of federal taxation was controversial. In fact, many did not believe that the 16th Amendment would garner the three-fourths majority needed for passage.[3] If not for the prospect of a global conflagration finding the United States without a standing military, the tax debate may have been further protracted.

Whether taxes are good or bad from a normative perspective is somewhat of a moot point. They are a reality. Tax collectors have historically been reviled, and they receive particularly dishonorable mention in the Bible. Taxes from the British Empire were a partial (though as mentioned not the only) catalyst for the American Revolution. Nonetheless, most people agree that there should be some level of taxation.

Controversy does tend to center around the use of tax proceeds. Funds used to provide public goods are generally well received as a productive use of tax dollars. The military is a good example of this, as it provides a degree of security that could not be similarly provided by the private sector. Goods and services that could otherwise be produced by industry are a much more divisive channel for tax revenue. Health care falls into this bucket.

Degree of taxation is another point of debate. The United States follows a progressive tax system that imposes higher tax rates for higher earners such that higher income brackets pay more on both a nominal and percentage basis. There is an argument that this discourages work effort. Indeed, it does seem at least anecdotally that high tax rates have a deleterious effect on motivation.

Also controversial is the concept of "double taxation." Much like the U.S. criminal justice system prohibits double jeopardy for defendants, there is a parallel camp that believes income should not be taxed twice at both the corporate and individual level. This has led to the establishment of qualified dividend rates, pass-through entities, lower corporate tax rates, and other conciliations that attempt to alleviate this effect.

Character of income is yet an additional topic of significant discussion, especially among tax professionals. This concerns the different tax rates applied to income characterized as ordinary income, dividends, and capital gains. How income is classified within these characterizations is the primary mechanism that is critiqued.

Whatever your persuasion, the purpose of this tome is not to debate the merits of taxation or advocate for reform to the tax code. Here, we are concerned with managing an existing tax system to maximize value in the form of the entertainment provided by college athletics. To do so effectively, it is necessary to dig further into the evolution of the tax system to understand its intricacies and determine appropriate policies to avoid undue taxation.

What is relevant about the debate over taxes is that it has driven, and continues to drive, periodic changes and updates to the tax laws. These updates will be discussed here with a focus on the main 3 codifications of tax law that have been enacted over the last 85 years. Note that this is not an exhaustive discussion of every federal tax law passed, as that could fill up an entire book in and of itself and is further not germane to the topic at hand.

The Revenue Act of 1939 was the first in a series of three codifications leading up to the current tax code.[3] It is a sparse document mostly referencing prior law. Focusing on corporations, it imposed a flat tax of 18 percent on income greater than $25k, with a graduated tax on profits below that threshold. The Act also provided for a two-year net operating loss (NOL) carryforward, meaning that corporate losses could be used to offset up to two years of future taxable income. For individuals, the 1939 Act provided for taxes on compensation earned over time, along with taxes on estates, and it included provisions for charitable contributions for individuals and corporations.[4]

A much more comprehensive codification was provided by the IRC of 1954. It is 372 pages and organized into 7 subtitles from A to G.[5] The IRC discusses income taxes, estate and gift taxes, employment taxes, and taxes on alcohol and tobacco, as well as other levies. It set forth procedure and administration and created the Joint Committee on Internal Revenue Taxation.[5]

The 1954 IRC also included substantial updates to the tax laws impacting individuals. Filing categories—including single, married filing separately, married filing jointly, and head of household—were created by the IRC. It also codified the progressive income tax with a table of over 20 tax brackets from 20 percent to 91 percent. The IRC also distinguished between short- and long-term capital gains and ordinary income.

Important in the 1954 manifestation of the tax code was its provision for a 25 percent flat tax on corporations going forward. Also relevant to our discussion was the 1954 IRC's establishment of tax-exempt organizations and the criteria for being treated as such. In addition, it included the concept of unrelated business taxable income (UBTI), which will be an important topic later.

Proponents of higher taxes often point to the 1954 IRC and its top marginal tax rate of 91 percent. The rate applied to incomes over $200k, which would equate to almost $800k in 2024 dollars. For individuals in the highest as well as other income brackets, the IRC provided for generous treatment of passive income loss deductions that taxpayers could avail themselves of. The result was that high earners, rather than paying taxes at the exceptionally high marginal rates, often paid no taxes at all.

While the IRC of 1954 effectively codified a disjointed precedent of tax laws, its length and complexity created substantial loopholes, which were often abused. Its open-ended treatment of deductions caused its unreasonably high and numerous tax brackets to backfire and actually reduce revenue generation. The need for reform catalyzed the passage of the IRC of 1986, which forms the bulk of the present-day tax code.

The IRC of 1986, which is now known as The IRC or Title 26 of the U.S. Code,[6] provided for 3 important changes to the 1954 IRC: (1) It reduced the number of individual tax brackets to 5 from 24, eliminating the notorious 91 percent rate and replacing it with a top rate of 39.6 percent. (2) The amended IRC placed limitations on passive income loss deductions. (3) The 1986 version of the IRC contained an important change to Section 501 of Subchapter F of the 1954 IRC, that was inserted by interim legislation and concerned exempt organizations—the focus of this publication.

For individuals, the most impactful reform of the 1986 IRC was the reduction in the number of income tax brackets and the curtailment of the top income tax rate. Offsetting this were new restrictions on passive income loss deductions. Passive loss deductions were an often-abused loophole in the 1954 IRC. They allowed individual taxpayers to offset their actively earned income with passive losses incurred in investments made in corporations, many of which were set up for the expressed purpose of generating a loss. In the IRC, there is now a distinction between regular income and passive income, with passive losses only eligible to offset the latter.

The 1986 Tax Code reduced and simplified taxes for individuals while eliminating abusive deductions that allowed savvy taxpayers to pay little or no income tax on their earnings. It is often credited with accelerating the economic boom of the 1980s and was a major political accomplishment for President Ronald Reagan. Notwithstanding these merits, our primary concern is with the advent of codified exemptions for nonprofits in the 1954 Code and with a change that occurred between the 1954 Code and 1986 Code as a result of interim legislation.

In addition, the Tax Cuts and Jobs Act, which was signed into law by President Trump, also made significant changes to the IRC. The law increased the standard deduction, reduced individual income tax rates across the board, lowered the corporate tax rate from 35 percent to 21 percent, and limited individual taxpayer deductions for state and local taxes.[2] It also made a notable change relevant to this discussion as it regards UBTI. This will be discussed in detail in a later chapter.

Key takeaways from this chapter:

1. Federal income tax on individuals and corporations was prohibited by the U.S. Constitution until the 16th Amendment in 1913.
2. The tax code has progressed through three major codifications in 1939, 1954, and 1986.
3. The 1986 Tax Code contained important changes made by interim legislation to the section of the IRC involving tax-exempt organizations.

2

Exempt Organizations

Starting even before the Revenue Act of 1913 was the concept that certain organizations and individuals should be exempt from federal taxation. Modern day examples of exempt individuals include military personnel while forward deployed, and exempt organizations are typified by churches and charities. This concept is based on the premise that entities performing a vital positive function for society should not be further burdened by taxation. We will focus this discussion on exempt organizations.

The United States maintains a robust charitable sector, with 1.8 million entities contributing $1.4 trillion to GDP in 2022.[1] This represents average annual growth of 5.9 percent over the last 47 years from its $94 billion contribution to GDP in 1975.[2] The sector is also the third-largest private employer in the country and grows at four times the rate of the for-profit private sector.[1]

Such explosive growth in the significance of charities to economic output has been driven in part by the expansion of the types of organizations that are considered charities. The Tax Code of 1939 contained scant discussion on exempt organizations. This was greatly expanded in the Tax Code of 1954 and carried over with some important changes leading up to the Tax Code of 1986, which substantially comprises the current code.

Herein, we will examine the evolution of exempt organizations in the tax code, with a focus on the exemptions used by college athletic organizations. This will show how intercollegiate sports obtained charitable status and lead into the discussion of the issues they face as a result. Through this understanding, we can provide effective strategies for retaining this status going forward.

U.S. tax law lists 25 types of nontaxable groups.[3] Most are described in Subchapter F of Chapter 1 under Subtitle A, Section 501, which contains the crux of the tax code's delineation of exempt organizations. The types of organizations that qualify for exemption have, like many aspects of tax law, changed with the various iterations of the IRC.

Three main categories of exempt entities are detailed in Section 501 of Subchapter F of the U.S. tax code. These include organizations qualifying under Sections 501(c)(1), 501(c)(2), and 501(c)(3). They are summarized as such:

Section 501(c)(1)—corporations organized by Congress to operate as arms of the federal government;

Section 501(c)(2)—corporations organized for the exclusive purpose of holding
title to and managing property for an exempt organization; and
Section 501(c)(3)—corporations organized exclusively for charitable causes.

For the purposes of this discussion, it is important to clearly define certain terms
that are often used interchangeably to describe exempt organizations. "Nonprofit"
refers most correctly to an entity's category of incorporation under state law as
opposed to federal tax status. "Exempt" organizations are those that qualify for
exemption from federal taxation under Section 501 of the IRC. It is critical to note,
however, that while many nonprofits qualify for exemption from paying federal
taxes on their own income, only charities in Section 501(c)(3) that are also scheduled
in Section 170 of Subchapter B on computation of taxable income are eligible to
receive tax-deductible contributions.

This is a crucial distinction, as the ability to solicit tax-deductible donations is a
major driver of fundraising capability. Individuals contributing to qualified 501(c)(3)
organizations enjoy the double benefit of supporting a worthy cause, as well as the ability to subtract their donation from their taxable income for the year, thereby reducing
their tax liability. Without this additional benefit, fundraising becomes exponentially
more difficult. Contributions to political organizations, which are not tax deductible,
are a mere fraction of the funds received by the charitable sector on an annual basis.

Section 170 describes the categories of corporations that are eligible to be listed
by individuals and corporations as itemized deductions for a charitable contribution. We will define these entities as proper "charities" for the remainder of this publication, clearly distinguishing them from the more generic "nonprofit" nomenclature,
as well as from the broader category of "exempt" organizations. As it concerns college sports, we will equate "exempt status" going forward to its current charitable
exempt status unless otherwise noted. Section 170 provides a definition of "charitable contribution" that is taken almost verbatim from the language defining qualification for tax exemption in Section 501(c)(3). Therefore, an organization exempt
under Section 501(c)(3) is essentially by default qualified to receive tax-deductible
donations under Section 170.

Charitable status as a 501(c)(3) organization is an invaluable designation. Not
only does it preclude an entity from generating federal tax liability through its operations, but it also enables it to offer a coveted deduction to prospective donors. The
value of this deductibility increases in direct proportion to one's tax bracket with
high earners gaining more value from a given deduction due to their higher marginal
tax rate. Individuals with high income are also more likely to itemize their tax
returns as opposed to taking the standard deduction under which charitable contributions are not deducted. Status as a charity therefore puts an organization squarely

in the spotlight of the highest earners who both itemize their taxes and have a great deal to gain from the deductibility of a donation.

Appealing to the wealthiest donors is a prerequisite for fundraising success, as capital campaigns are by nature distributed in a bimodal manner characterized by many very small and very large donations. To the extent that smaller donations are of any significance, they are more likely to be catalyzed by matching offers on behalf of one or more big donors. Most funds generated from these campaigns are therefore accounted for by a small number of substantial donations. These individual mega donations would likely be unattainable without deductibility, especially as they are often a product of estate planning.

As a result, achieving and maintaining status as a proper charity is mission critical to the success of an organization that relies on donations to fund its activities. It is hence incumbent upon the leadership of these organizations to pay close attention to Section 501(c)(3) and its requirements. To fail to do so would jeopardize the future of the entity going forward.

The genesis of the exempt organization language in the current tax code dates to the Tax Code of 1954, where Section 501(c)(3) makes its first appearance. In the section that follows is the exact text from the Tax Code of 1954:

Sec 501: Exemption from Tax on Corporations, Certain Trusts, Etc.[4]

(c) List of Exempt Organizations. – The following organizations are referred to in subsection (a):

(3) Corporations, and any community chest, fund, or foundation, organized and operated exclusively for religious, charitable, scientific, testing for public safety, literary, or educational purposes, or for the prevention of cruelty to children or animals, no part of the net earnings of which inures to the benefit of any private shareholder or individual, no substantial part of the activities of which is carrying on propaganda, or otherwise attempting, to influence legislation, and which does not participate in, or intervene in (including the publishing or distributing of statements), any political campaign on behalf of any candidate for public office.

From the aforementioned text, it is apparent that the Tax Code of 1954 lists a number of charitable pursuits that qualify for tax exemption. For the most part, the list is uncontroversial. Religious, scientific, and educational organizations, including groups that prevent cruelty to children and animals, provide a clear positive benefit to society and deserve to carry out their functions without the burden of taxation. It is through the educational organizations stipulation in Section 501(c)(3) that college sports enjoy one of their two exemptions, as they are sponsored by institutions of higher education.

Moreover, the Tax Code of 1954 rewards certain beneficent endeavors with the ability to solicit tax-deductible donations under Section 170 (c)(2):

Sec. 170. Charitable, Etc., Contributions and Gifts.[4]

(c) Charitable Contribution Defined. – For purposes of this section, the term "charitable contribution" means a contribution or gift for the use of –

    (2) A corporation, trust, or community chest, fund, or foundation –

        (B) Organized and operated exclusively for religious, charitable, scientific, literary, or educational purposes or for the prevention of cruelty to children or animals;

As such, Section 170 of the Tax Code of 1954, which delineates what qualifies as a "charity" for the purposes of deductibility from individual and corporate taxes, certifies substantially all of the exempt functions listed in Section 501(c)(3) as properly charitable. This makes the tax deductibility qualification under Section 170 nearly interchangeable with Section 501(c)(3).

The symmetry of Section 170(c)(2)(B) and Section 501(c)(3) is important, as many exempt organizations are excluded from what is defined as a charity. These include organizations qualifying under Sections 501(c)(4) to (16) such as civic leagues, labor organizations, fraternal societies, and credit unions. The activities mentioned as follows are deemed sufficiently altruistic for exemption from taxes but not socially beneficial enough to warrant acceptance of tax-deductible charitable contributions.

The following is a list of exempt functions that do not qualify as charities scheduled by their subsection within Section 501(c): [4]

  (4) civic leagues or local associations of employees;

  (5) labor, agricultural, or horticultural organizations;

  (6) business leagues, chambers of commerce, boards of trade;

  (7) clubs organized for recreation and other nonprofit purposes;

  (8) fraternal beneficiary societies, orders, or associations;

  (9) voluntary employees' beneficiary associations;

(11) teachers' retirement fund associations;

(12) benevolent life insurance associations;

(13) credit unions;

(14) mutual insurance companies; and

(15) corporations organized for the financing of crop operations.

Certain of the pursuits in 501(c) are discussed in Section 170, such as domestic fraternal societies, orders, and associations operating under the lodge system, wherein contributions are permitted deduction only to the extent used for one of the properly scheduled charitable purposes. This essentially doubles down on the language affirming the charitable functions in 501(c)(3). Two other types of organizations—war veterans' groups and cemetery companies—are given specific mention as qualifying charities.

The bifurcation of exempt organizations into charitable and noncharitable status is rational from the point of view of federal tax revenue generation. Foregoing tax collections from a specific source has a quantifiable impact on overall tax income. Conversely, permitting additional sources of taxation to be shielded by virtue of their donation to an already exempt source can have a multiplicative effect on inflows. Therefore, the universe of charitable organizations that can solicit deductible contributions is defined very narrowly.

Under this system, while your local credit union does not pay taxes on its profits, you cannot walk into a branch and make a donation that will be deductible against your personal income taxes. As noted previously, there are many types of organizations that have this hybrid status as tax-exempt groups that are not charities. Nonetheless, you can walk into your church, temple, or school and make a contribution that can be written off on your tax return, as these are proper charities.

Charitable status is functionally an exclusive club that avails its members of vast fundraising capabilities. Membership criteria for this elite group have remained relatively constant over the last 70 years. Nonetheless, there was a meaningful change in the time that elapsed between the Tax Code of 1954 and the Tax Code of 1986 that prevails today. This change furthermore has significant implications for the discussion at hand.

To understand this change to the IRC, it is necessary to rewind to the 1970s and the era of the Cold War. During this period, the United States and the Soviet Union competed fiercely in nearly every domain except for the battlefield. This included arts, sciences, economics, the space race, international athletic competition, and virtually every type of nonmilitary pursuit in addition to the obvious competition for the number and sophistication of nuclear and conventional weapons.

Against this backdrop was the Montreal Summer Olympics in July 1976. The games are known for the African boycott involving 22 countries in protest of New Zealand's participation, given that its rugby team had toured Apartheid South Africa.[5] More relevant to our discussion is that the U.S. gold medal count of 34 was dwarfed by the 49 taken home by the Soviet Union.[5] Something clearly needed to be done to improve our performance in international sports.

The U.S. Senate viewed this country's less than stellar performance in the Olympics as stemming from a lack of funding to organizations whose purpose was to cultivate talent for international competition.[6] Specifically identified were two types of organizations:[7]

1. "national organizations "responsible for the conduct of national and international competition, including the conducting of national championships and the selection of national teams in Olympic and Pan American sports;" and
2. "national, local, and regional organizations whose primary purpose is supporting and developing amateur athletes for participation in national and international competition in Olympic and Pan American sports."

The result was the Tax Reform Act (TRA) of 1976, which amended Section 501(c)(3) to exempt certain groups that fostered amateur athletic competition from federal income tax.[7] These organizations would further be added to Section 170 to allow for deductibility as charities. Through this amendment to the IRC, it was hoped that amateur athletic organizations would be sufficiently capitalized with tax-deductible contributions to train the next generation of Olympic athletes and therefore equip the United States to better compete with the Soviet Union on the international sports stage. It also had the collateral impact of providing intercollegiate athletics with another means of exemption from federal taxation.

Following the amendment introduced by the 1976 Act, the text of Section 501(c)(3) that carried over into the 1986 and current Tax Code reads as such (with changes from the 1954 Code underlined):[7]

Section 501. Exemption from Tax on Corporations, Certain Trusts, Etc.

(c) List of exempt organizations

(3) Corporations, and any community chest, fund, or foundation, organized and operated exclusively for religious, charitable, scientific, testing for public safety, literary, or educational purposes, or to foster national or international amateur sports competition (but only if no part of its activities involve the provision of athletic facilities or equipment), or for the prevention of cruelty to children or animals, no part of the net earnings of which inures to the benefit of any private shareholder or individual, no substantial part of the activities of which is carrying on propaganda, or otherwise attempting, to influence legislation (except as otherwise provided in subsection (h)), and which does not participate in, or intervene in (including the publishing or distributing of statements), any political campaign on behalf of (or in opposition to) any candidate for public office.

Just as in the 1954 Code, Section 170 parrots Section 501(c)(3) in providing for deductibility of the charities scheduled in the latter section:[7]

Section 170. Charitable, Etc. Contributions and Gifts

(c) Charitable contribution defined

For the purposes of this section, the term "charitable contribution" means a contribution or gift to or for the use of-

(1) A State, a possession of the United States, or any political subdivision of any of the foregoing, or the United States or District of Columbia, but only if the contribution or gift is made exclusively for public purposes.

(2) A corporation, trust, or community chest, fund or foundation –

   (A) created or organized in the United States or in any possession thereof, or under the law of the United States, any State, the District of Columbia, or any possession of the United States;

   (B) organized and operated exclusively for religious, charitable, scientific, literary, or educational purposes, <u>or to foster national or international amateur sports competition (but only if no part of its activities involve the provision of athletic facilities or equipment)</u>, or for the prevention of cruelty to children or animals.

   (C) no part of the net earnings of which inures to the benefit of any private shareholder or individual; and

   (D) which is not disqualified for tax exemption under section 501(c)(3) by reason of attempting to influence legislation, and which does not participate in, or intervene in (including the publishing or distributing of statements), any political campaign on behalf of (or in opposition to) any candidate for public office.

Note: as in the 1954 Code, Section 170(c) also lists war veterans organizations and cemetery companies, along with fraternal societies (subject to the same restrictions).

As such, the 1976 Act codified amateur sports organizations as charities exempt from income tax and eligible to solicit tax-deductible contributions. It is important to note that Congress had a specific intent with this amendment, and that was to support the development of Olympic athletes. As stated in the Senate Congressional Record: "it is not intended to make social clubs, or organizations of casual athletes, into tax-exempt charities. Only an organization whose primary purpose is the support and development of amateur athletes for participation in international competition in Olympic and Pan American sports will qualify under this amendment. Organizations whose primary purposes are the recreation of their members or whose facilities are used primarily by casual athletes will not qualify."[7]

The intent to disqualify the broader universe of athletic organizations beyond those fostering national and international competition may have been the impetus behind the language proscribing the provision of athletic equipment and facilities. From the record, however, it is unlikely that Congress contemplated the use of this exemption by higher education to shield its athletic activities from taxation.

Nevertheless, it is apparent that the TRA of 1976 has had a substantial impact that goes far beyond the preparedness of the United States for international Olympic competition.

What is made abundantly clear in the language inserted into Section 501(c)(3) by the 1976 TRA is that the exemption applies only to "amateur" sports organizations. Professional athletic leagues are therefore specifically excluded. Furthermore, non-professional leagues that are involved with the provision of athletic equipment and facilities are likewise disqualified from exemption.

Before the 1976 Act, Congress had described Section 501(c)(3) as a "source of confusion and inequity" for organizations engaged in training athletes for international competition.[7] Clearly, the intent of the Act was a strategic attempt to improve U.S. standing in world athletics during a time period when success in all categories of international competition was considered essential for winning the cultural contest between the East and the West. It is, however, not unfounded that the spirit of the exemption provided by the TRA of 1976 would be capitalized on by college sports since, as discussed in a later chapter, they are today the primary breeding grounds for Olympic athletes.

Nonetheless, given that the exemption is being used on the peripheries of its original intent, vigilance should be exercised to maintain standing under it. This would include refraining from the provision of athletic equipment and ensuring that the athletic activities engaged in remain amateur in nature and do not cross over into the world of professional sports. Ostensibly, these stipulations should be easy to conform to.

A key question that emerges is that given the large stadiums and courts in and on which college teams play, college athletics does have an equipment provision component to it; does this void their exemption? Fortunately, the addition of IRC 501(j) specifically eliminated this requirement, and thus organizations are free to provide athletic equipment without interfering with their exemption under Section 501(c)(3).

Prior to the TRA of 1976, educational institutions could nonetheless avail themselves of the educational exemption in 501(c)(3). This has historically been the most often cited reason for exemption. However, the size and scope of college athletics was exponentially smaller in the world prior to mass media and, as such, today the educational exemption is likely predicated on college sports at least failing to qualify as professional. We delve into this issue herein, and an important part of understanding it relates to the historical evolution of college athletics, which is discussed in the next chapter.

Key takeaways from this chapter:

1. Section 501(c)(3) of the tax code was changed significantly by the TRA of 1976, which provided exemption for organizations that foster athletic competition.
2. The updated language in the IRC specifically requires exempt sports organizations to be amateur in nature.
3. As we will see in the next chapter, the size and scope of college athletics has expanded to a point where it must depend on this exemption to avoid taxation and its consequences.

3

Evolution of College Athletics

The first college founded in the United States was Harvard in 1636.[1] It was followed shortly thereafter by William & Mary in 1693[1] and subsequently proceeded by Yale, University of Pennsylvania, Princeton, and others in the 18th century. Significant institutions of higher learning, such as my alma maters Hamilton College and the University of Virginia (UVA), made their way into the world in the 1800s.

Initially, the purpose of these establishments was to educate clergy.[2] Indeed, the first presidents of both Harvard and William and Mary, Increase Mather and James Blair, respectively, were preachers. The former played a prominent role in the Salem witch trials. Outside of clerical training, the clear intent of higher education was to increase students' understanding of the Bible.[2]

Under the religious bend of early colleges and universities, life was austere and banal. Puritan philosophy discouraged games of all types, and the celebration of Christmas and Easter was proscribed. This was certainly not a fertile environment for the development of athletic competition.

As a result of the pious orientation of the first cohorts of post-secondary schools, athletics did not become a principal part of campus life until the 19th century. It started with the installation of gyms to promote health and to provide a distraction from the mischievous and rebellious activities of students at the time.[3] By the 1840s, people were engaging in football, baseball, and cricket.[3] These games, however, were not organized and were infrequent.

In 1843, boat clubs at Harvard and Yale were formed making rowing the first organized college sport.[3] Competition between schools ensued, and the newly created College Rowing Association held regattas in 1860.[3] Ultimately, the impetus for the emergence of formalized college athletics was an inferiority complex with the British, who were considered to be in better shape and more athletic than their college-aged U.S. counterparts.[3] This Anglophile aspect of the development of college athletics will have relevant implications down the road.

Some also credit the Civil War with enshrining the institution that is college football in the South today, with the first game played on April 9, 1880 on Old Stoll Field at the University of Kentucky.[4] It became an outlet in the former confederate states for frustrations following defeat in the war. The game combined elements of rugby into an innovative contest prosecuted on a gridiron field. Its appeal was supported by its likeness to combat with Charles Daly of the U.S. Military Academy, referring to it in 1921 as a "war game."[4]

By the end of the 19th century, a number of sports—including cricket, baseball, rowing, track and field, and football—were popular college pastimes. In particular, football became the foundation for the future of college athletics. It was soon to be joined by basketball, which was invented in the United States by James Naismith in 1891. The new sport moved quickly to the South, with Vanderbilt playing at the Nashville YMCA only two years later in 1893.[4]

The late 19th century was also the beginning of the oldest U.S. athletic conference. Purdue President James Smart and the leaders of seven midwestern universities met at the Palmer House hotel in Chicago to create the Intercollegiate Athletic Association.[5] This later became the Big Ten.

As the United States entered the 20th century, college athletics also underwent a transition. Early football was violent and involved mass formations, gang tackling, and pile on situations that often resulted in the loss of life. During the 1904 season alone, 18 deaths and 159 serious injuries resulted from the sport, prompting President Theodore Roosevelt to advocate for new regulations.[6] He called the leaders of Harvard, Princeton, and Yale to the White House to reform the game. However, during the 1905 season, deaths and injuries continued to increase.[6]

In response to this crisis, New York University (NYU) chancellor Henry MacCracken pulled together 13 schools to reform football rules. On December 28, 1905, 62 colleges and universities became charter members of the Intercollegiate Athletic Association of the United States (IAUS), which was the precursor to the NCAA.[6] It was officially constituted as the rule-making body for college sports in May 1906.

The turn of the century also saw the first bowl game. The Rose Bowl was initiated in 1901, with Michigan playing Stanford.[7] The result was a lopsided score of 49-0 in Michigan's favor. This may explain why the game was not played again for 14 years. In 1907, the Missouri Valley Conference was formed, making it the second oldest Division I conference.[8]

College sports began the second decade of the 20th century with renewed vigor under the auspices of its newly created regulator. On December 29,1910 the IAUS was renamed the NCAA. In 1914, the Yale Bowl opened with a Harvard versus Yale football game. In 1915, The Rose Bowl reappeared and continued its existence to this day as an annual event.[7] The Pacific Coast Conference (PCC) also began around this time, with four schools as charter members—the University of California at Berkley, the University of Washington, the University of Oregon, and the Oregon

Agricultural College (now Oregon State).[9] They were joined by Washington State College in 1917 and Stanford in 1918.

The Roaring Twenties saw the first NCAA-sponsored championship, a national collegiate track and field tournament at the University of Chicago. In 1922, the PCC added the University of Southern California (USC) and the University of Idaho and then further expanded to 10 teams with the addition of the University of Montana in 1924 and UCLA in 1928.[9] In 1927, a 22-year old inventor named Philo Farnsworth created the first prototype of a fully electronic television.[10] This breakthrough would later have an exponential impact on the growth of college sports, albeit twenty years later.

Four bowl games were launched in the 1920s. These included the Fort Worth Classic (1920), the San Diego Classic (1921 and 1922), the Dixie Classic (Dallas in 1921 and 1924), and the Los Angeles Christmas Festival (1924).[7] These events made only brief one- or two-off appearances. It wasn't until the 1930s that certain of the perennial bowl contests appeared. In 1928, the University of Kansas, the University of Nebraska, the University of Missouri, Iowa State, and Kansas State separated from the Missouri Valley Conference to form the Big Six, which would ultimately grow to become the modern Big 12.[11]

In 1934, the Orange Bowl and Sugar Bowl premiered in Miami and New Orleans, respectively.[7] The year 1935 witnessed the beginning of the Sun Bowl in El Paso, Texas and in 1936, the Cotton Bowl started in Dallas.[7] The Dixie Classic came back in 1933, and the Bacardi Bowl was played a handful of times in Batista-controlled Havana, Cuba.

The Southeastern Conference (SEC) was formed in 1933. It originally consisted of 10 schools: Alabama, Auburn, Florida, Georgia, Kentucky, LSU, Mississippi, Mississippi State, Tennessee, and Vanderbilt.[4] These schools were part of the Southern Intercollegiate Athletic Association, which began meeting in 1894.

The year 1937 saw the birth of the National Association of Intercollegiate Athletics (NAIA), a competitor to the NCAA.[12] It currently oversees college athletics at 250 member institutions, which are comprised of smaller colleges and universities.[13] Total student athlete enrollment stands at 83,000 across 28 sports.[13]

Also in the 1930s, the National Invitational Tournament (NIT) was founded in 1938.[14] The first NCAA Division I men's basketball tournament was played in 1939, consisting of eight teams.[14] During this time, the term "March Madness" was first used by an Illinois high school official to refer to basketball. It would not become affiliated with the tournament until many decades later.

World War II created a new dynamic for college sports, particularly for football. With many teams sidelined due to the pool of available players serving in the military, the military itself fielded teams that competed with some of the premier names in the sport. These included the Fort Knox Armoraiders, the Iowa Pre-Flight Seahawks, and others who played blue chip programs such as Notre Dame, Michigan, and Ohio State.[15] Legendary Alabama coach Bear Bryant served as an assistant coach with the Georgia Pre-Flight Skycrackers and the North Carolina Pre-Flight Cloudbusters.[15]

In addition to the Pre-Flight schools, which prepared pilots for service, there were the V12 naval officer training programs, which seconded personnel to colleges and universities.[16] These trainees were eligible for football, so many school programs staffed their teams with cadets, albeit often with changing rosters.[16] This created a big role for the Navy in college football. Unfortunately, some schools who could not field teams were forced to switch to eight-man football, and others ended up quitting the sport altogether.

The NCAA basketball tournament continued to be played throughout the war. From 1941 until 1945, it featured matchups with Wisconsin and Washington State, Stanford and Dartmouth, Wyoming and Georgetown, Utah and Dartmouth, and Oklahoma State and NYU.[14] Perhaps because of its smaller rosters, basketball, unlike football, was not dependent on the military for players. The finals did feature an uncanny number of schools traditionally perceived as more academic focused such as Dartmouth, Stanford, and Georgetown, most of whom (with the exception of Georgetown during the Patrick Ewing era) would never be seen again in the title game. The tournament would enjoy uninterrupted play for 81 years until it was canceled for the first time in 2020 due to the COVID-19 pandemic.

Many bowl games were activated post–World War II. These included the Gator Bowl in 1945; the Raisin (1945–1949) in Fresno, California; the Oil (1945 and 1946 in Houston); the Great Lakes (1947 and 1948); the Shrine (1948–1951 in Phoenix); the Harbor (1947–1949 in San Diego); the Delta (1947 and 1948 in Memphis); and the Dixie (Bowl, not Classic, in 1947 and 1948 in Birmingham, Alabama). Two one-time bowls were played that later resurfaced: the Alamo (1946 in San Antonio, Texas) and the Camellia (1948 in Lafayette, Louisiana). In 1948, the Big Six became the Big Seven, when Colorado joined.[11]

In the 1950s, the postwar U.S. economy enjoyed robust growth, which ushered in the advent of new technologies that U.S. citizens increasingly capitalized on to enjoy sports. Television, which was invented in the 1920s and became commercially available in the 1930s, was not aggressively marketed until after the war and saw widespread adoption in the 1950s.[17] Among sports watched on TV, baseball was the most popular of the professional leagues, while in college, football dominated the scene.

Two additions to the bowl schedule in the 1950s included the Liberty Bowl—which was played in Philadelphia from 1959 to 1963 and in Atlantic City in 1964 before moving to Memphis in 1965—and the BlueBonnet Bowl in Houston in 1959. The final two Salad Bowls were played in 1950 and 1951, and a one-time Presidential Cup in College Park, Maryland occurred. In 1959, the PCC was dissolved, and the Athletic Association of Western Universities was formed, which ultimately adopted the name Pacific 8.[9] Oklahoma State joined the Big Seven in 1959, making it the Big Eight.[11] In the NCAA Tournament, the number of teams doubled to 16 in 1951.[6]

The 1950s also set the stage for what was, up until that time, one of the biggest scandals in college sports. The Metropolitan New York Athletic Conference— which included teams such as City College of New York (CCNY), NYU, and Long Island University (LIU)—enjoyed enormous popularity, with games regularly selling out in Manhattan's Madison Square Garden.[18] In 1950, City College became the first team to do the previously unthinkable and win both the NIT and the NCAA Tournament.[18] This phenomenon would ultimately blow the lid off a pernicious under-trend in college sports—point shaving.

Particularly acute to basketball due to its high scoring games, this form of corruption involves players, officials, and others who conspire to alter the final game tally to enrich gamblers who bet on the points spread. In this way, a team that is favored to "cover" the spread can be artificially made to underperform, allowing those betting on the other side of the equation to achieve windfall gains. The team that ultimately wins or loses is not necessarily impacted, which can create the unrealistic impression that this is a victimless crime.

In 1951, the scheme was unveiled when Junius Kellog, a Manhattan College basketball player, reported to the New York County District Attorney's office that he had been offered a $1,000 bribe to shave points during a future game at Madison Square Garden.[19] As it turns out, organized crime figures, gamblers, and other malfeasants had been grafting players and officials for years to fix upward of 86 games involving 32 players from 7 colleges. These included CCNY, LIU, NYU, Manhattan College, University of Kentucky, Bradley University, and the University of Toledo.[19]

The aftermath of what was really the first major scandal in college athletics was many criminal prosecutions and the imposition of severe penalties by the NCAA. A total of 10 fixers were sentenced to prison terms stretching as long as 12 years.[19] Seven CCNY players received suspended sentences, and a putative first-round draft pick who would have played for the Knicks, Sherman White from LIU, served nine months in jail and was barred from the National Basketball Association (NBA).[19] Kentucky basketball received the dreaded "death penalty," one of the first teams to do so, with its 1952 and 1953 season canceled while LIU completely mothballed its athletics department for six years.[19] Unfortunately, this would not be the last scandal to tarnish college sports.

In the 1960s, television took off as the primary medium by which spectators experienced college athletics. We will return to this trend in the next chapter, and the significant impact it will have on the manifestation of college sports in the United States. The 1960s also saw the beginning of the Peach Bowl in Atlanta and the Tangerine Bowl in Orlando, Florida that is now known as the Citrus Bowl.

The year 1961 witnessed the revelation of an additional basketball cheating scandal, this one featuring NYU in a starring role. In similar fashion to the 1951 fiasco, the 1960s version involved the collusion of organized crime and basketball players to fix games and generate gambling revenue. All in all, 37 players from 22 schools were charged in connection with the scheme with NYU at the epicenter.[18] The events led to the dissolution of the Metropolitan New York Conference.[18] Already reeling from the events of 1951, which also involved NYU, the university ultimately canceled its basketball program completely in 1971, citing budget constraints.[20] It was reinstated in 1983; however, it was in Division III, where it remains to this day.

Yet another cheating scandal broke in the 1970s, this one dubbed the "Boston College Point Shaving Scandal." Beneficiaries of this racket included three Pittsburgh gamblers and a New York City mobster and involved three Boston College players who allegedly accepted money to fix games during the 1978–1979 season.[21] The subsequent federal trial spawned the ESPN film *Playing for the Mob*.

The NCAA created the divisional structure that exists today in 1973, which categorizes sports as Division I, II, or III.[6] The divisions are meant to create a reasonable competitive environment for teams by grouping colleges together based on the size of their enrollments and athletics departments. Today, the median Division I school has an enrollment of 8,960, with a median of 2,428 for Division II and 1,740 for Division III.[6] Division I schools are required to maintain at least 6 sports for men and 8 sports for women and play nearly all of their games against other Division I opponents.[22] Division II institutions must provide at least 5 sports for men and 5 for women, or 4 for men and 6 for women, with football and basketball required to play at least 50 percent of their games against Division II or higher teams.[22] The biggest distinction between Division III and the other divisions is that Division III colleges and universities do not offer athletic scholarships.

The 1978 season was a watershed year for college football, as Division I was subdivided into Division I-A and Division I-AA at the NCAA convention in Atlanta.[23] The genesis of this schism, which only affected football, was similar to the calculus behind current conference realignments—schools with larger programs wanted to disintegrate from those with a less significant or nonexistent football presence. The original criteria to compete in the more prestigious Division I-A included maintaining at least a 30,000 seat stadium; having average attendance of 17,000 over the last 4 years or for 1 year in the last 4 years; and playing at least 60 percent of games against other I-A teams.[23] Notwithstanding these criteria, schools could qualify for I-A if they had a 12-sport program versus a minimum 8-sport lineup while meeting qualifying standards.[23]

Motivation for the divisional split extended beyond revenue sharing. More importantly, the larger schools wanted autonomy from burdensome regulations often favored by smaller institutions. These included stipulations that limited scholarships and placed caps on the size of coaching staffs along with a litany of recruiting guidelines.[23] Ultimately, the makeup of Division I-A approximated 79 schools from the 7 top conferences and independents, along with 25 schools admitted under the so-called "Ivy League Amendment" for programs that included 12 intercollegiate sports and 65 in Division I-AA.[23]

The year 1972 marked the point that the federal government passed landmark legislation in the form of Title IX of the Education Amendments. This statute barred federally funded institutions from engaging in discriminatory conduct on the basis of sex. For college sports, this meant providing opportunities to women for athletic participation in proportion to their representation in enrollment. This led to a significant expansion in the number of women's sports offerings at colleges and universities.

Other than these happenings, the 1970s also included the birth of the Fiesta Bowl in 1971 in Tempe, Arizona and the Independence Bowl in 1976 in Shreveport, Louisiana. The number of teams in the NCAA Tournament doubled again to 32 in 1975.[6] In 1978, the University of Arizona and Arizona State University joined what then became the PAC-10.[9] The Big East Conference was founded in 1979 with Providence, St. John's, Georgetown, Syracuse, Seton Hall, Connecticut, and Boston College as the seven charter members.[24] In the 1970s, another significant event in NCAA history occurred that will be discussed in the next chapter.

In 1981, the Big Ten endorsed a proposal to enable their women's intercollegiate programs to affiliate with the conference. The first women's conference championship happened that fall. The 1980s also saw the beginning of the NCAA women's basketball championship with the first tournament played in 1982.

During coverage of the 1982 men's college basketball tournament, CBS announcer Brent Musberger first used the term "March Madness" to refer to the tournament. The NCAA obtained a trademark for this moniker in 2001.[25] The tournament's official anthem "One Shining Moment" was written by David Barrett in 1986 and first used in the men's basketball tournament in 1987.[26] In 1985, the tournament's current 64 team single elimination format was adopted.

In the final decade of the 20th century, some conference realignments occurred with the University of South Carolina and the University of Arkansas joining the SEC in July of 1991.[4] The NCAA opened its new headquarters in Overland Park, Kansas in 1990, only to move again in 1999 to Indianapolis, the site of its current headquarters.[6] In 1992, the NCAA formed its Gender-Equity Task Force, which is tasked with studying the treatment of male versus female athletes.[6]

The Bowl Championship Series (BCS) began in 1998.[6] Controversial from its beginning, the BCS involved a selection committee that would choose the two teams that would play for the college football national championship. The committee typically considered a team's position in two long-standing polls—the AP Poll and the Coaches Poll—to determine who would play in the title game.

Originally, the national championship rotated among the four most significant bowl games: the Rose Bowl, the Orange Bowl, the Sugar Bowl, and the Fiesta Bowl. These were coined "BCS Bowls," because they could alternatively be the host for the national championship. This practice continued until 2007 when a separate BCS National Championship game was added to the schedule for the two teams playing for the ultimate title.

Significant controversy erupted during the 2003 season, when Oklahoma, which ranked third in the AP Poll, was selected to play in the Sugar Bowl BCS National Championship over the top-ranked team USC. The fiasco resulted in a split national championship, with LSU winning the BCS, while USC was considered to be the champion by the AP.[6] Controversy continued to envelop the BCS for the next decade until it was discontinued in 2013.

In 2006, Division I-A and Division I-AA changed their names to the Football Bowl Subdivision (FBS) and Football Championship Subdivision (FCS), respectively. To compete in the FBS, teams must maintain a minimum average home game attendance of 15,000 for at least 1 year in a rolling 2-year period.[22] FCS teams do not have to meet attendance requirements, and football schools not qualifying for FBS are essentially in FCS by default.

Also in 2006, a collective bargaining agreement between the National Basketball Players Association and the NBA resulted in the now infamous "one-and-done" rule.[27] Under this new regulation, the minimum draft age was raised to 19, meaning that players would need to complete 1 year of college or at least be 1 year removed from high school before entering the NBA. The rule would have a significant impact on college basketball from that point on, encouraging elite players to join college teams for a single season before declaring for the draft.

The second decade of the 21st century bore witness to many conference realignments. The PAC-12 emerged in 2010 as the University of Utah and former Big 12 member University of Colorado joined the PAC-10.[9] In 2012, Missouri and Texas A&M also defected from the Big 12 and joined the SEC, which grew to a 14-school membership.[4] The ACC added Syracuse University, the University of Pittsburgh, the University of Louisville, and the University of Notre Dame, sans football, in 2013 as all of these schools left the Big East.[11] The Big Ten, never one to change its name, also expanded to 14 schools as it added the University of Nebraska in 2011 and the University of Maryland and Rutgers in 2014.[11]

Clear winners from the 2010s conference shakeups were the SEC, the ACC, and the Big Ten, which netted significant additions to their memberships. Otherwise affected were the Big East and the Big 12, whose structures shifted dramatically following the realignment. The Big East had already been hemorrhaging schools since the departure of the University of Miami, Virgnia Tech, and Temple in 2004 and Boston College in 2005. In December 2012, before the mass exodus from the conference, DePaul, Georgetown, Marquette, Providence, St. John's, Seton Hall, and Villanova formed an independent association that severed ties with the FBS members and retained the Big East name and partnership with Madison Square Garden to host the conference tournament.[23] As such, the Big East has persisted over the last 10 years as a basketball-only conference. The Big 12 departures were partially offset by the addition of West Virginia and Texas Christian University (TCU).[11] Despite being reduced to 10 members, the conference has kept its name unchanged.

Similar to the divisional split decades prior, the impetus behind the conference jockeying boils down to revenue sharing among members. For schools with large programs, particularly in football, there is an incentive to associate with similarly endowed institutions versus those with less successful or nonexistent offerings. This trend has continued to this date with conference changes becoming more common and frequent.

The year 2011 witnessed what was likely the most significant scandal in college sports to date. In November of that year, Jerry Sandusky, a former defensive coordinator for Penn State football, was arrested on 40 criminal charges involving sexual abuse of minors. Penn State Coach Joe Paterno, Athletic Director Tim Curley, and President Graham Spanier were alleged to be complicit in covering up years of misconduct by Sandusky, resulting in multiple children being victimized.[28] Paterno, although cleared of criminal culpability by the Pennsylvania Attorney General, was fired by the board of trustees along with Graham Spanier. Spanier and Curley faced criminal charges for failing to report the abuse. Paterno died in January of the next year following a rapid deterioration in health following his firing.

When the scandal broke, there was widespread speculation that Penn State could receive the "death penalty" from the NCAA and have its football program canceled for one or more seasons. Ultimately, however, they faced a $60 million fine, a reduction in scholarships, and a 4-year postseason ban. In addition, 111 of Joe Paterno's wins were vacated. The NCAA later lifted the bowl ban in 2014, and Paterno's wins were restored. Sandusky is currently serving a prison sentence of 30–60 years.

Penn State unfortunately presents an archetype for alleged conduct that prioritized program goals, including winning and revenue, over ethical behavior. Scandals such as this one have sadly been part of the impetus for undermining the institution that college athletics is in the United States. Unlike the typical recruiting transgressions and other violations of the myriad rules promulgated by the NCAA, this incident involved actual criminal conduct that jeopardized the safety and soundness of individuals unaffiliated with the program, who in this case happened to be minor children. Going forward, if it is not too late, college athletics will need to avoid headlines of this nature for its own survival.

In 2013, the BCS was discontinued in favor of the College Football Playoff (CFP). In this new format, a selection committee chooses four teams from the FBS to play in two semifinal playoff games that rotate annually among the Cotton Bowl, Fiesta Bowl, Orange Bowl, Peach Bowl, Rose Bowl, and Sugar Bowl.[29] The two winners of these Playoff Semifinals go on to compete in the CFP National Championship that is held in a different city each year on a Monday night. The CFP moved to a 12-team playoff format in the fall of 2024.

The year 2014 saw a very interesting story come out of the University of North Carolina at Chapel Hill (UNC-Chapel Hill). This differed from prior revelations in that it was essentially a hybrid of an academic and an athletic scandal. Student athletes were allegedly taking independent study courses that were graded in an overly favorable manner. An example of a paper submitted in such a class leaked, along with its high grade, despite the fact that it was an obviously low-quality production. The situation resulted in UNC-Chapel Hill's accreditor, the Southern Association of Colleges and Schools, putting it on probation, a status from which it was released a year later.[30]

While benign relative to situations involving criminal conduct, this type of headline also presents more complexities than regular way allegations of rule violations, because it crosses into another discipline. It is another sort of occurrence that needs to be avoided, lest there be a legitimate claim that college athletics in a wholesale fashion compromises the academic integrity of educational institutions. This is something that can be particularly disconcerting to faculty who at many colleges and universities play an active role in governance through mechanisms such as a faculty senate. Resultingly, although not a violation of criminal codes, this type of transgression can create support for regulations on campuses—and, as we have seen, in the law—that are unfavorable to athletics.

Conversely, what happened at Baylor in 2016 involved very serious criminal allegations. The world's largest Baptist university, Baylor was the focus of a U.S. Title IX investigation that year following allegations of rape by Baylor football and rugby players.[31] These sexual assaults, some of which were purported to be gang rape in style, left 15 victims who recently settled their federal lawsuit with the university.[31] In the wake of the revelations, President Ken Starr of Clinton special prosecutor fame and football coach Art Briles were fired.[31]

Baylor's strict protocol on alcohol and fraternization did little to mitigate the circumstances and, based on some of the claims, further exacerbated the situation by deterring victims from coming forward. One person close to this situation saw it stemming from a lack of oversight at the top of athletics departments, which can become fiefdoms that too easily overlook red flags. It may also just be that bad actors can manifest themselves in any environment. Whatever the underlying cause of these circumstances, it is once again the type of occurrence that college athletics needs to desperately avoid.

The year 2018 heralded the beginning of the transfer portal for athletes. Prior to this development, student athletes would be enjoined from participating for one year following a transfer to another institution. This "redshirt" year regulation was designed to prevent the development of an active secondary market for players whereby coaches could poach talent from other teams.[32] Exceptions to this policy would often be granted by the NCAA in situations such as the departure of a coach. Under the new regulations, students can complete the transfer module and become eligible for recruitment by other schools where they would be permitted to compete immediately in their program.[32]

The year 2022 began the first year of the NCAA's new Name, Image, and Likeness Policy, commonly referred to by its acronym NIL. For decades, there had been controversy over the use of athletes' names and images in commercial realms such as video games without any compensation going to the athlete. NIL ended that and for the first time permitted college athletes to be renumerated for the use of their name, image, or likeness. For many, this would mark the first time they would derive material monetary benefit for their participation in college athletics prior to joining a professional league.

With NIL and other developments over the last decades, college athletics has entered a new phase. In this phase, extraordinary diligence will be required to avoid the potential for severely adverse tax consequences for the college sports industry. In subsequent chapters, we further analyze the challenges this U.S. institution faces and provide recommendations for avoiding highly negative outcomes.

Key takeaways from this chapter:

1. College athletics has had a storied history going back more than a century and a half. Interspersed with the tribulations of intercollegiate competition have been, like in any industry, scandals of varying severity.

2. Certain scandals, such as those involving criminal conduct or undermining the academic pillar of higher education, are particularly malignant in that they can result in adverse policy consequences for college athletics.

3. With the emergence of NIL and other significant changes, college athletics has entered a new phase where diligence will be required in order to prevent potentially catastrophic tax treatment.

Genesis of the Problem

As mentioned in the last chapter, television was invented in the 1920s, but its adoption was delayed until after World War II. In the immediate postwar period, household television sets were sparse, and storefronts and bars provided for public viewing places.[1] Programs were of poor quality, and other mediums of visual entertainment such as Broadway theater and vaudeville were preferred. By 1948, television was still an experimental technology, and radio dominated the airwaves.

Even in its nascent phase, college athletics was an integral part of television. Games were programmed throughout the 1940s, and many popular matchups were moved to weekends to encourage households to purchase sets.[1] Nonetheless, it remained a popular pastime for fans to gather in pubs and in front of stores to catch events, especially football games.

In 1934, the Federal Communications Commission (FCC) replaced the Federal Radio Commission as the governing federal agency for broadcast media.[2] As the primary regulator for television, the FCC would play a meaningful role in its evolution, many times in a controversial way. In the 1940s, as television was taking hold, it made some of its first significant actions.

Television's rapid growth trajectory was creating conflicts with different signals interfering with each other. Although the big three networks—ABC, CBS, and NBC—had leveraged their market share in radio to create a similar oligopoly for television, the transmissions that ultimately reached end users had to be carried by local affiliates. Proliferation of these local allocations was crowding the airwaves, so regulatory action was deemed necessary. In 1948, the FCC put a freeze on new television station licenses.[2] Although intended to be a temporary ban, it was not lifted until 1952.[2]

The 1950s was largely considered to be a golden age for television. The United States was experiencing a booming postwar economy, and TV was becoming an increasingly relevant part of people's lives. The 1952 presidential campaign was the first played out on television and became famous for slogans such as "I Like Ike," referring to candidate and ultimate 34th President Dwight D. Eisenhower. It was also known for quirky political anecdotes such as the Nixon "Checkers" speech, whereby the then-vice-presidential running mate diffused allegations of accepting improper contributions by admitting his dog was a campaign donation that he would not return.[3] This was also the time of the Red Scare, and, as such, there was concern that television could be used as a mechanism for spreading communist propaganda. In the midst of this scare, a number of television personalities were accused of being communists and discredited.[1]

Television took off in the 1960s. Average daily household TV viewing surged to more than five hours per day, with radio listening down to less than two hours.[4] The iconic Nixon-Kennedy debate reached 70 million viewers and is credited with handing Kennedy an early victory. Nearly 90 percent of U.S. households had televisions at this time.[1] Movie theater attendance plunged, and it was here that the controversy surrounding television for time immemorial began to emerge. Programs were considered of low intellectual caliber and advertisements misleading. This set the stage for government agencies to regulate content going forward.

One of the FCC's overriding mandates has been to enforce decency standards in broadcasting. This originally began with a form of moral suasion by the agency for networks to adopt a self-regulatory regime whereby certain content, such as violent programming, would be relegated to the post 9:00 p.m. time frame.[1] This would allow other time slots to be made available for family-oriented content or at least material that would be harmless to younger viewers.

Despite its storied history, college athletics has always enjoyed the advantage of being beyond reproach for its suitability to a wide variety of audiences. Athletics in general enjoys broad appeal to adults of different demographics, yet contests typically do not contain anything that could be objectionable from a decency standpoint. (We will except the controversies surrounding the Ultimate Fighting Championship and Mixed Martial Arts from this discussion as they came later.) This makes the sports industry highly compatible with broadcast media across the spectrum of time slots available.

In fact, in the early days of the FCC, the commission included sports in its 14 "major elements" of programming that were a necessity for the public interest, which included:[5]

> "1 Opportunity for local self expression. 2 the development and use of local talent, 3 programs for children, 4 religious programs, 5 educational programs, 6 public affairs programs, 7 editorialization by licensees, 8 political broadcasts, 9 agricultural programs, 10 news programs, 11 weather and market reports, 12 sports programs, 13 service to minority groups, 14 entertainment programs."

College athletics in particular has typically presented a more sanitized version of sports vis-à-vis that of professional leagues. Until recently, alcohol was not served at games (albeit sometimes with the opposite of the intended effect), and standards of conduct were theoretically enforced at a higher level in facilities managed by educational institutions. The amateur designation has further contributed to the purist image of the college athlete.

The compliance of college athletics with decency standards would ultimately be a significant driver of its success in the world of visual media. Combined with the influence of regulatory agencies on the development of broadcast television, this would make sports one of the most sought-after forms of programming. In this way, it is apparent that regulation in general has had a positive effect on the success of college sports.

In a broadening of their mandate, the FCC further sought to regulate the source of broadcast programming. With the three major networks dominating the medium, the regulators looked to limit their influence by encouraging independent programming. The result would provide a further boost to college athletics and sports in general in the burgeoning television market.

The agency had, in the past, taken action against what it believed was an overconcentration of influence in a handful of companies. In 1941, the FCC imposed a regulation that prohibited the ownership of more than one radio network by a single company. Subsequently, NBC divested its Blue Network, which became ABC.[1]

In 1971, the Prime Time Access rule went into effect, which limited the major networks to three hours of captive programming from 7:30 p.m. to 11:00 p.m.[1] Coincident with this rule, the Financial Interest and Syndication Rules ("fin-syn") were introduced, which enjoined the networks from participating financially in anything other than wholly owned programs.[1]

As explained by the Federal Trade Commission in its hearing before the FCC on the fin-syn rules in 1990:[6]

> "The Commission's Financial Interest and Syndication ("Fin-Syn") Rules limit broadcast networks' ability to integrate vertically in the sale and distribution of syndicated programming. Specifically, the rules prohibit the networks from engaging in the domestic syndication of any program or the foreign syndication of any independently-produced (i.e. nonnetwork produced programs). The rules also prohibit the networks from obtaining any financial interest, or proprietary right or interest, in the exhibition, distribution, or use of programs produced by others, except for the exclusive right to network exhibition in the United States."

These regulations therefore paved the way for the rise of independent content in television, including college sports. It also prevented the networks from acquiring an early and controlling interest in formats that would later explode in popularity and value. As an agreeable and independent form of content, college sports was ideal material for a new industry that would come to dominate mass media.

Leading the charge into the world of television for college athletics was its lead regulator, the NCAA, which had come into existence with much fanfare at the turn of the century. Beginning in the postwar era, the NCAA would be the point organization for the negotiation of television rights and the mechanism for the distribution of proceeds from these arrangements. It would serve in this capacity for nearly four decades.

In the beginning, television was initially viewed as a competitor for in-person attendance. We see this today in certain markets where broadcast coverage is blacked out if turnout at the venue of competition is deemed too thin. This is despite the fact that in the immediate postwar environment, most households did not own a television. As such, the alternative to attending a game would be to watch it in a storefront window or at a bar.

Nonetheless, gate receipts were in decline and college football, which had enjoyed a renaissance after World War II, was beginning to suffer as some institutions abandoned the game due to its expense.[1] As a result, in 1951, the NCAA officially took control of broadcasting rights and began imposing regulations to limit the amount of airtime that teams could accumulate.[1] This created immediate conflict with certain schools, such as the University of Pennsylvania and Notre Dame, with preexisting agreements with networks to televise games.[7]

An outright ban on TV coverage of games by the NCAA was challenged by Penn and others who ultimately backed down under the threat of repercussions.[7] Over time, the NCAA relaxed its restrictions, initially allowing sold-out games to be televised, and then providing for one national game to be broadcast each week in 1952, before permitting NBC to cover regional games in 1953.[7] By 1955, NCAA regulations allowed for one national game to be televised for eight weeks and for regional games to be on TV for five weeks.[7]

Amid the regulatory burden of the NCAA, the independent bowl games were growing in popularity and success, convincing educational institutions that television was an auspicious environment for college athletics.[7] These divergent views on the value of live broadcasts would set the stage for a dramatic shift in leadership on the issue. In many ways, it was the genesis of the problem facing the industry today.

As the relationship with broadcasting grew, there was from the outset fractiousness among institutions of different sizes on the matter of revenue share.[1] Larger schools with expansive programs and massive attendance believed they deserved the lion's share of the proceeds. Smaller institutions felt that the big programs could not exist in a vacuum, and therefore they were entitled to a portion of the revenue. Moreover, given the fact that small schools, by their sheer number, represented most of the members, they dominated NCAA decision-making through their votes.[1]

The dichotomy between revenue generation and political power within the NCAA led to the creation of separate divisions for universities and colleges in 1968; 223 were categorized as the former and 386 as the latter.[1] Subsequently, in 1973, the creation of Divisions I, II, and III in the NCAA discussed in the previous chapter occurred. As we now know, this did not put an end to the contention over revenue share.

In 1977, the SEC, the Big Ten, and the other major football conferences, got together to form the College Football Association (CFA) as a competitor to the NCAA for the purposes of television rights sponsorship.[1] The split of Division I into I-A and I-AA for football purposes was done largely in response to the creation of the CFA.[1] Notwithstanding, the lines were being drawn up for a battle between the large football schools and the NCAA.

Unappeased by the divisional split, the CFA attempted to establish its own broadcasting rights contract in 1981.[1] Catalyzed by threats of retaliatory action by the NCAA, CFA members University of Georgia and University of Oklahoma, along with a separately acting University of Texas, filed federal lawsuits against the NCAA.[1] The suits alleged violation of the Sherman Antitrust Act.

The Sherman Antitrust Act was passed in 1890 and represented the first federal legislation banning monopolistic business practices.[8] Monopolies are considered "conspiracies in restraint of trade" and disrupt markets by concentrating power in a unitary participant versus fostering competition among independently acting parties. The legislation has been used in the past to break up monopolies such as Standard Oil and AT&T. In this context, the CFA lawsuits alleged that the NCAA was essentially a monopoly and that conspiring officials were unfairly stifling competition by restraining the ability of individual institutions to negotiate television contracts for themselves.

In 1984, the Supreme Court agreed with the plaintiffs in the matter of *NCAA v. Board of Regents of University of Oklahoma*, and by a vote of 7-2 affirmed a lower court decision, which had described the NCAA as behaving as a "classic cartel."[9] The CFA lawsuits had found their way to the nation's highest court and prevailed. In writing the opinion of the court that affirmed the District Court's ruling, Justice Stephens stated:[9]

> "The NCAA plays a critical role in the maintenance of a revered tradition of amateurism in college sports. There can be no question but that it needs ample latitude to play that role, or that the preservation of the student athlete in higher education adds richness and diversity to intercollegiate athletics and is entirely consistent with the goals of the Sherman Act. But consistent with the Sherman Act, the role of the NCAA must be to preserve a tradition that might otherwise die; rules that restrict output are hardly consistent with this role. Today we hold only that the record supports the District Court's conclusion

that, by curtailing output and blunting the ability of member institutions to respond to consumer preference, the NCAA has restricted, rather than enhanced, the place of intercollegiate athletics in the Nation's life. Accordingly, the judgment of the Court of Appeals is *Affirmed.*"

By its decision, the Supreme Court ended the NCAA's control over television revenue. It therefore freed up individual institutions and conferences to negotiate their own television rights agreements. By disintermediating the NCAA from football television revenue, the decision also severely undermined the NCAA's ability to act as an overriding regulator for college athletics given its estrangement from a substantial amount of monetary flow.

Today, most of the NCAA's revenue, by far, is derived from its Division I men's basketball tournament, over which it retains control through a number of trademarks. These include "March Madness," "Road to the Final Four," and other phrases. In its fiscal year ended August 2023, the NCAA men's tournament generated $873 million from its television and licensing rights agreement with CBS and Turner Broadcasting.[10] This represented just under 76 percent of the NCAA's total revenue from operations that year of $1.15 billion, which excludes roughly $150 million of investment gains.[13] In addition to the tournament, the NCAA also earns money from the televised contests of "nonrevenue" sports such as volleyball, cross country, and lacrosse.[11]* It receives no intake, however, from regular season basketball games and conference tournaments, as those fall under the purview of the conferences.

When the NCAA was at the helm of broadcast contract negotiations, television revenues grew more than tenfold, from $3 million in 1961 to $31 million in 1981, before doubling to $62 million in 1982, the final year of NCAA control.[1] This represented annual growth of nearly 15 percent. During roughly the same period, physical attendance increased at an average rate of less than 3 percent per year. As such, this lends further credibility to the assertion that television was the true engine of growth and that the NCAA's efforts to protect attendance by restricting TV exposure were misguided.

After the NCAA relinquished infinite control over television rights, conference revenues grew exponentially. In 2023, the "Power 5" conferences combined to generate $3.6 billion in total revenue from their media rights contracts.[12] The breakdown is as follows:[12]

Big Ten: $879.9 million;
SEC: $852.6 million;

---

* For 2023, this includes the women's basketball tournament. Starting in the 2024–2025 season, $65 million will be specifically allocated to the women's game.[14]

ACC: $707.0 million;

Pac-12: $603.9 million; and

Big 12: $510.7 million.

These dramatic gains in intake have nonetheless failed to quell the dispute over revenue share. Conference realignments, once 100-year events, are now occurring with regular frequency. As revenue has increased and been concentrated under the control of the conferences, there has been a commensurate increase in the incentive to align with the ones that are in the most lucrative circumstances.

In the summer of 2024, these dynamics remained highly active with turnover in nearly all of the major five conferences. USC and UCLA are leaving the Pac-12 for the Big Ten, while Oklahoma and Texas are exiting the beleaguered Big 12 to join the SEC.[12] To mitigate these losses, the Big 12 extended invitations that were accepted by Houston, UCF, BYU, and Cincinnati.[12]

Driving these maneuvers is the divergence in economics among the media deals that the respective conferences have negotiated. The Big Ten leads the pack with its 7-year agreement with NBC, CBS, and Fox Sports signed in 2022 that is valued at over $7 billion, one of the largest grossing contracts in college sports to date.[12] In 2020, the SEC signed a 2024–2034 media rights contract with ESPN worth $3 billion.[12] It is therefore no surprise that they have both been net winners in the recent realignments.

With its new additions, the Big 12 was able to extend it preexisting arrangement with Fox Sports and ESPN through 2031 that is expected to generate $2.3 billion.[12] As the final season of its current deal with ESPN and Fox came to a close, however, the Pac-12 remained without a contract. This no doubt reflects the disruption created by the departures. Even as this book goes to print a long term agreement for the conference remains up in the air.

The ACC remains well positioned, as it is only midway through its exclusive 20-year deal with ESPN.[12] Nonetheless, there have been grumblings within the conference. At issue is the concept of equal revenue share that remains the standard in college sports conferences.

In the post-NCAA administered world ushered in by the Supreme Court antitrust decision, the various conferences—such as the SEC, ACC, Big Ten, Pac-12, Big 12, Mountain West, and so forth—are the primary arbiters of television revenue contracts. This provides significant pricing power, as the conferences can bundle a large mass of content and negotiate an arrangement to distribute it, often with some type of exclusivity. A notable exception to this is Notre Dame football, which has its own media rights contract with NBC and is independent for football purposes, although for all other sports, it is a member of the ACC.

As conduits for media broadcasting revenue, the conferences divide up the proceeds among their members. The predominant formula for this to date has been equal share. In 2023, the SEC, with 14 members, distributed $51 million to each school for proceeds for that year; the Big Ten $58.8–60.5 million per institution; the ACC $43.3–$46.9 million; the Pac-12 $33.6 million; and the Big 12 $43.8–$48.2 million per school.[12] This represents an impressive average cash distribution margin of just less than 90 percent.

To their credit, the conferences are run very efficiently, subsisting on relatively lean payrolls and budgets. On its website, the ACC lists a staff of roughly 50, the SEC denotes 54, and the Big Ten has 78.[13] Comparatively, a professional services organization with a top line of $500 million would typically have upward of 3,000 employees.[2] This is consistent with the conferences' primary purpose as aggregators of media revenue, although it is less conducive to a regulatory role.

Still, high-performing schools and programs are likely to continue to lobby for a percentage of distributions that more closely reflects what they feel is their contribution to the financial performance of the conference. For them, equal revenue share provides disproportionate benefit to schools whose programs do not produce as much air-time quality content. Expect this to drive further disagreement and conference shuffling going forward.

What is more important for this discussion, however, is not how the money is distributed, but rather what it is used for. Based on Knight Commission reporting, most of FBS conferences' expenses are allocated to facilities and equipment (roughly 20 percent), followed by coaches' compensation (also around 20 percent) and then support and administration (slightly less than 20 percent). Athletic student aid hovers around 10 percent for these organizations, and the remaining 30 percent is spread over a myriad of expenditures for game travel, recruiting, competition guarantees, and other expenses.[14]

Media rights represent a plurality of the revenue earned by the large conferences. They further have a highly synergistic impact on other streams of renumeration, such as corporate sponsorships. As we will discuss in a later chapter, they are not the only source of funds for college athletic programs.

No matter what the origin, all sources of college athletics revenue earned by the NCAA, the conferences, and the individual academic institutions share one major commonality—they are all tax free. This is despite the fact that almost none of the aforementioned uses of proceeds are particularly charitable. The money remains tax free by virtue of the educational purpose of the member institutions that sponsor the programs and by the exemption provided for amateur athletics in Section 501(c)(3) of the IRC that was inserted by the TRA of 1976. As will be discussed, these two exemptions have a symbiotic relationship with each other that it is critical for college athletics to preserve going forward.

In a world where these exemptions did not exist, the concept of UBTI enters the equation. This is the topic of the next chapter.

Key takeaways from this chapter:

1. College athletics has been highly compatible with television as a form of mass media, representing decent and independent content.
2. The Supreme Court's antitrust decision in 1984 decoupled the NCAA from most television revenue.
3. All sources of revenue for college athletics, including media rights, are free of taxes due the exemptions offered to educational institutions and amateur sports.

UBTI[1]

UBTI is not well understood, even among those relatively familiar with finance and taxation. The concept dates back at least 74 years and has wide- ranging effects today. It is essentially taxable income received by an otherwise exempt entity or in a qualified account. Pension funds and charities, as well as IRAs, are all susceptible to exposure to UBTI.

Prior to the 1950s, charities could generate revenue from activities directly related to their charitable mandate, as well as from peripheral endeavors that did not directly correspond to their mission.[2] The only prerequisite to avoiding taxation was for the money to ultimately be used to further its charitable purpose.[2] This raised concern about competitive fairness in that charities could significantly undercut for-profit private sector companies that were subject to taxes. In addition, many of these charities were not required to file returns with any information on these side businesses, making them essentially black boxes.[1]

The Senate Finance Committee concluded that:[1]

> "The problem at which the tax on unrelated business income is directed is primarily that of unfair competition. The tax-free status of IRC Section (501) organizations enables them to use their profits tax-free to expand operations, while their competitors can expand only with the profits remaining after taxes."

Tax on unrelated business was imposed by the Revenue Act of 1950. For tax years after 1950, this applied to most charitable organizations with some exceptions. It required exempt entities to pay taxes on income derived from business activities not directly related to their charitable purpose. The tax rate imposed was the prevailing corporate tax rate.

These taxes would continue to evolve with additional changes to the tax code. The most recent change came in 2017 and actually presents some relevance to this discussion. UBTI, as it is now called, is a critical tax phenomenon for college sports, as it will impact a plethora of groups involved in the industry in the event it loses its *ipso facto* exemptions. A comprehensive background on this aspect of the tax code is therefore provided in this chapter.

Subtitle A, Chapter 1, Subchapter F, Part III, Sections 511 to 515 of Title 26 of the U.S. Code contain the text for the imposition of taxes on unrelated businesses. They directly follow Section 501(c)(3), which outlines the criteria for charitable status, and these sections are highly interrelated. UBTI limits the scope of 501(c)(3) activities to those that directly align with charitable purposes.

Section 511, which came from the 1950 Act, introduces taxes on unrelated business income:[3]

§511. Imposition of tax on unrelated business income of charitable, etc., organizations

(a) **Charitable, etc., organizations taxable at corporation rates**

    (1) **Imposition of tax**

There is hereby imposed for each taxable year on the unrelated business taxable income (as defined in section 512) of every organization described in paragraph (2) a tax computed as provided in section 11. In making such computation for purposes of this section, the term "taxable income" as used in section 11 shall be read as "unrelated business taxable income."

    (2) **Organizations subject to tax**

        (A) **Organizations described in sections 401(a) and 501(c)**

The tax imposed by paragraph (1) shall apply in the case of any organization (other than a trust described in subsection (b) or an organization described in section 501(c)(1)) which is exempt, except as provided in this part or part II (relating to private foundations), from taxation under this subtitle by reason of section 501(a).

        (B) **State colleges and universities**

The tax imposed by paragraph (1) shall apply in the case of any college or university which is an agency or instrumentality of any government or any political subdivision thereof, or which is owned or operated by a government or any political subdivision thereof, or by any agency or instrumentality of one or more governments or political subdivisions. Such tax shall also apply in the case of any corporation wholly owned by one or more such colleges or universities.

As a note, the Revenue Act of 1950 made exceptions for certain groups such as churches. This was followed by a belief that many of these excepted organizations were abusing their status and delving into unrelated businesses. The TRA of 1969 proceeded to impose a tax on the unrelated business income of essentially all organizations exempt from taxes under 501(c)(3). In addition, state colleges and universities had at one point been excepted from UBTI under the Revenue Act of 1950. This was eliminated by the Revenue Act of 1951 and, as such, Section 511 reads as it does. As stated in Section 511(a)(2)(B), this tax extends to wholly owned subsidiaries of state colleges and universities as well.

Section 512 sheds further light on what is considered a UBTI:[3]

§512. Unrelated business taxable income

(a) **Definition**

For purposes of this title—

(1) **General rule**

Except as otherwise provided in this subsection, the term "unrelated business taxable income" means the gross income derived by any organization from any unrelated trade or business (as defined in section 513) regularly carried on by it, less the deductions allowed by this chapter which are directly connected with the carrying on of such trade or business, both computed with the modifications provided in subsection (b).

Section 513 also provides for a definition of an unrelated business:[3]

§513. Unrelated trade or business

(a) **General rule**

The term "unrelated trade or business" means, in the case of any organization subject to the tax imposed by section 511, any trade or business the conduct of which is not substantially related (aside from the need of such organization for income or funds or the use it makes of the profits derived) to the exercise or performance by such organization of its charitable, educational, or other purpose or function constituting the basis for its exemption under section 501 (or, in the case of an organization described in section 511(a)(2)(B), to the exercise or performance of any purpose or function described in section 501(c)(3)).

Through Sections 511–513, the IRC sets forth the criteria for UBTI. Based on the IRC, three qualifications are necessary for income to be deemed UBTI. These include:

1. The income is derived from a trade or business.
2. Such trade or business is regularly carried on by the entity or organization.
3. Said trade or business is not substantially related to the entity or organization's exempt purpose.

The IRC defines the term "trade or business" in Section 162 as part of its delineation of itemized deductions for expenses. In the opinion of the IRS, this includes "any activity carried on for the production of income from the sale of goods or performance of services."[1] Further, legal precedent sets a standard for an activity's constitution as a trade or business as whether it "was entered into with the dominant hope and intent of realizing a profit," with profit motive defined as "an intent to generate receipts in excess of costs."[1]

In case law and regulation, the concept of a trade or business has been heavily refined to a precise definition. Its parlance has been revisited so frequently that activities are subject to disaggregation from larger operations and can be classified as a trade or business even as a component of a broader endeavor that lacks profit motive. This is known as the "fragmentation rule." An example of this rule in case law is provided by *United States v. American College of Physicians, 475 U.S. 834*, where the court ruled that the sale of advertisements by an exempt organization in a publication related to its charitable purpose nonetheless constituted a trade or business that was unrelated to its mission and therefore subject to taxation.

Moreover, it is the position of the IRS that activities that do not generate a profit are not necessarily declassified as trades or businesses. This is especially true if they were entered into with the intent of earning a profit that ultimately did not materialize. In addition, a lack of intent to compete with for-profit businesses is not considered a viable defense to being categorized as a trade or business.

It is therefore apparent that the first prerequisite for UBTI can be applied to a vast universe of activities, including those one would not normally associate with a trade or business. Given the amount of revenue generated by college athletics, it clearly would qualify as a trade or business, regardless of the ultimate profitability or the fact that it is a component of a broader institutional education effort.

Regarding the second criterion for UBTI—that the trade or business be "regularly carried on" as per Section 512—the IRS pursues a temporal approach to this definition. In general, activities are considered regularly carried on if they "manifest a frequency and continuity and are pursued in a manner generally similar to comparable commercial activities of nonexempt organizations."[1] In this way, year-round activities certainly qualify as being regularly carried on. Temporary activities, however, do not meet this definition. An example would be a lemonade stand or canteen that was operated by a nonprofit for only a week or two in a year.

Revenue rulings, however, have created a broad categorization of activities that are considered to be regularly carried on. Specifically, the sale of advertising by an exempt symphony orchestra in its concert program that was distributed free at performances over an eight-week period was deemed to be a business that was regularly carried on. Conversely, the sale of advertising in a program for an annual charity ball was not determined to be an activity that was regularly carried on. Most relevant to our discussion is the case of a two-week horse race conducted by an exempt county fair that was determined to be a regularly carried on business, because it occurred with a frequency that mirrored for-profit horse races that are held in a specific season.

It is apparent from this precedent, therefore, that college athletics would be determined to be regularly carried on, as they occur with a periodicity that parallels the seasonality observed by professional athletic organizations such as the NBA, the National Football League (NFL), and other for-profit sports groups. Even if this were not the case, the seasons of most college sports comprise a sufficient percentage of the total year, as to be determined to be regularly occurring. In this way, college sports would fully meet the second criterion for UBTI if they were not intrinsically charitable.

On the final criterion for UBTI—that the activity in question not be "substantially related" to an organization's charitable purposes—we have some specific guidance from the IRS. In particular, the IRS requires an analysis of the relationship between the trade or business at hand and the mission of the exempt organization. In order to be substantially related, there must be a "causal" relationship between them. This precludes an incidental or peripheral association from qualifying as a substantial relationship.

Specifically, IRS literature states that income generating activities "must contribute importantly to the accomplishment of the organization's exempt purpose to be substantially related."[1] There is a large amount of case precedent provided by Treasury Regulation 1.513-1(d)(4)(i) to support this assertion. The conclusions vary depending on the circumstances, as well as the charitable missions of the featured organizations. Some activities may be substantially related to certain exempt purposes but not to others.

In one example, a school's physical education department ran a ski slope for instructional use as well as for the recreation of its students and paying members of the general public. In this revenue ruling, the recreational use of the facility by the students was determined to be substantially related, because it contributed importantly to the school's tax-exempt purpose. Use of the slope by the public, however, was deemed to be an unrelated trade or business.

In another case, a state university owned two noncommercial radio stations, as well as a television broadcasting operation that was commercially sponsored. It was determined that the commercial television station was an unrelated business. Further, the university was enjoined from deducting expenses from the noncommercial operations that were determined to be substantially related to the university's exempt purpose from the for-profit income of the disallowed television station.

A Section 501(c)(5) agricultural group whose charitable purpose was to improve conditions of breeding operations of Angus cattle and improve the breed was determined to be engaged in an unrelated business when it sold cattle for its members on commission. This conclusion was determined based on the fact that the sale of the cattle did not produce any benefit to breeding conditions or to the breed itself. Such sales therefore did not contribute importantly to the exempt organization's purpose.

Several decades ago, a Section 501(c)(3) charity dedicated to the prevention of cruelty to animals was determined to be sponsoring an unrelated business by providing pet boarding and grooming services. It was decided that such services did not advance the purpose for which the organization qualified as a charity. The income from boarding and grooming was therefore subject to UBTI.

Later, it was decided that the operation of beauty shop and a barber shop for senior citizens by a Section 501(c)(3) senior center was not an unrelated business. The activity was determined to "meet the psychological and health needs of the elderly in the area of personal grooming." Income from the beauty shop and barber shop was not subject to taxation.

A Section 501(c)(4) homeowner's association (HOA) that owned parking lots and a beach club that were exclusive to members during the summer was hit with UBTI, as the operations were declared unrelated businesses. The lots and club were remote from the subdivision by eight miles and were not open to the public. As such, they did not relate to the HOA's exempt purpose of promoting general public welfare.

Additionally, facilities that are used for exempt purposes can generate taxable income when dual purposed for noncharitable activities. In furtherance of this, a museum with a theater that shows educational programming would be operating an unrelated business if and when that theater is used to show regular way motion pictures. A school whose tennis courts are used by a tennis pro for a tennis camp would be required to allocate the rental income from the pro as an unrelated business.

Advertising revenue has historically been a big target for UBTI. In one example, a charity that published an annual yearbook was declared to be generating UBTI via its advertising campaign whereby it received a portion of the proceeds. In addition, a law enforcement agency that sold space in its journal was deemed to be operating an unrelated business and subject to tax. Also, a professional association that sold subscriptions to its membership for a periodic journal was determined to not be subject to UBTI for that activity, because it contributed substantially to its exempt purpose.

However, the same organization was determined to be subject to UBTI on its sale of advertisements in its journal. Additionally, a classical music charity that owned a radio station was required to pay UBTI on commercial advertisements sold on its airtime.

Endorsements have also been singled out as an abuse of exempt status. An example of this is provided by a scientific group that was decided to be exploiting its reputation and charitable designation by selling endorsements of laboratory equipment to for-profit manufacturers. A bar association was also charged UBTI for commercial products and services advertised in its journal. Further, a trucking association that featured advertisements for truck products in its newsletter was ruled to be responsible for taxes on UBTI, as it did not editorialize on the products and employed no selection criteria for its commercial content.

This brings up an important point, as there is a royalty exemption in the tax code for charitable organizations. Specifically, IRC 512(b)(2) modified IRC 512(a) and excluded "all royalties (including overriding royalties) whether measured by production or by gross or taxable income from the property..."[1] Royalties have been defined as being a share of property and, as such, the IRS has held that a functional definition of "royalties" is that a royalty must (1) relate to the use of a valuable right and (2) be measured in some manner by the use that is made of that right.[1]

In precedent, attempts to shelter income that would otherwise be considered UBTI by categorizing it as royalties have met with minimal success. In particular, the IRS has held that income received by an exempt organization does not constitute royalties within the meaning of IRC 5(b)(2) if such income is compensation for services.[1] In one case, a Section 501(c)(3) organization that aided families of college students by working with travel agencies to plan trips received a per person fee from the travel agencies. This was determined to be payment for services versus a licensing or royalty fee for using the organization's intellectual property.

Moreover, prior revenue rulings have made it clear that income received from a partnership with or in a for-profit business cannot be considered royalties. In fact, the impact of a charitable organization partnering with a for-profit entity has significance beyond the issue of royalties. By their existence, these types of arrangements are likely incompatible with exemption under Section 501(c)(3), because the asserted charity could be used to promote the private interests of the for-profit group.

The Revenue Act of 1950 also specifically disallowed "feeder" organizations from exemption.[4] "Feeder" corporations consist of for-profit enterprises that distribute all of their proceeds to a charity. Under the current tax code, such income cannot be shielded from taxes and is considered UBTI. This will have serious implications for our future discussion on the scenario whereby previously exempt income becomes taxable.

It is therefore unlikely that college athletics could find a safe harbor in the royalties exemption if its revenue suddenly became taxable as UBTI. Certain income, such as sales of merchandise with institutional logos, could avail itself of this shelter, but most of it could not for various reasons that will be discussed. There is, however, one often-cited case that has been relied upon to quell concerns about the taxability of revenue generated from collegiate sports.

Revenue Ruling 80-296, 1980-2 C.B. 195 targeted the issue of whether the sale of broadcasting rights to an annual competitive intercollegiate athletic game by a Section 501(c)(3) educational organization fell under the definition of an unrelated trade or business, as per Section 513. In this case, the IRS ruled as follows:[5]

> "On the basis of the facts and circumstances presented in this case the educational purposes served by intercollegiate athletic activities are identical whether conducted directly by individual universities or by their regional athletic conference. Also, the educational purposes served by exhibiting a game before an audience that is physically present and exhibiting the game on television or radio before a much larger audience are substantially similar. Therefore, the sale of the broadcasting rights and the resultant broadcasting of the game contributes importantly to the accomplishment of the organization's exempt purposes."

Hereby, in 1980, this ruling reaffirmed college athletics' exemption under the educational organization category of Section 501(c)(3). The fact that this decision is 44 years old, however, makes educational value of questionable reliance today as a stand-alone exemption. At the time, college athletics had not reached nearly the size and scope that it has today. This is a critical point, given the establishment of Treasury Regulation 1.513-1(d)(3) in 1983 which specifically addressed the scale of activities peripheral to an organization's exempt purpose. This related to trade shows conducted by exempt organizations, stating that "where income is realized from activities that are conducted on a larger scale than is reasonably necessary for the performance of an exempt function, the income attributable to the excess constitutes gross income from the conduct of unrelated trade or business."[1]

Arguing that the modern manifestation of intercollegiate athletics is conducted on a scale that is commensurate with its educational purpose is difficult enough. It goes without saying that a professionalized version of the same would not pass the test of contributing importantly to an exempt purpose. In a scenario where college athletics was fully professionalized, the more logical conclusion would be that nearly all of the revenue generated by college athletics—from media deals and outside endorsements from for-profit entities—has no relationship to the educational purpose for which institutions of higher learning are exempt from taxes.

Treasury Regulation 1.513-1 postdates the 1980 ruling that seemingly exempts broadcast revenue from categorization as UBTI. Furthermore, in its "Exempt Organizations Technical Guide; TG 48: Unrelated Business Income Tax," with a revision date of December 15, 2023 (upon which this chapter is heavily based), the IRS had this to say about the 1980 ruling:[1]

> "The Service has traditionally taken the position that income from admissions to college and university athletic events isn't income from unrelated business because the events themselves are related to the educational purposes of colleges and universities."

The technical guide specifically states the position of the IRS on revenue generated from attendance at college athletic events, but it makes no mention of broadcasting rights. This may implicitly indicate an intent by the IRS to walk back the guidance from the 1980 ruling. We cannot know for sure, but it certainly does not inspire any confidence in reliance solely on educational purpose should college athletics become professionalized.

In 2017, the Tax Cuts and Jobs Act added further complication to the issue of UBTI. The Act amended Section 512(a) by adding Section 512(a)(6), which imposes the requirement for exempt organizations running multiple unrelated businesses to calculate the UBTI for each one separately.[1] This essentially gives discrete revenue streams from UBTI distinct characteristics from each other. NOLs must be determined and NOL carryforwards maintained separately for each business. Functionally, this precludes using losses from one unrelated business to offset the taxable income of another. We will discuss the importance of this change in a later chapter.

For the sake of thoroughness as it concerns the IRC, Section 514 relates to the applicability of UBTI to debt financed real estate transactions. Section 515 provides for the use of foreign tax credits against UBTI. The lack of relevance of these two sections to the topic at hand is the reason they have not been discussed in this chapter.

Therefore, the overall conclusion from this discussion on UBTI is that in order to maintain exemption from taxes, it is of the utmost importance for college athletics to remain nonprofessional. This concept of "nonprofessionalism" is the topic of the next chapter.

Key takeaways from this chapter are:

1. Organizations with charitable exemptions, such as colleges and universities, are nonetheless required to pay taxes on revenue streams unrelated to their charitable purpose.

2. In an environment where intercollegiate athletics is professionalized, it is unlikely that it would qualify as contributing significantly to the respective institutions' exempt educational purpose. Further, it would relinquish all or substantially all claims to exemption as fostering amateur sports and thereby dispossess itself of both exemptions.

3. To the extent that charitable organizations are determined to be the beneficiaries of multiple unrelated businesses, the income and taxes for each must be separately determined.

Nonprofessionalism

The concept and debate around amateurism in college sports extends back to the early 20th century. In the 1920s, it was common for college athletes to be sponsored to engage in competition.[1] Typically, these arrangements were controlled by alumni and not necessarily the educational institutions.

It was an environment certainly ripe for abuse, given its unregulated nature. As college football surged in popularity post–Word War II, the NCAA sought to impose some discipline on the process.[1] What they came up with became the precursor to the regulatory regime that ultimately dominated the industry.

Similar to many of the issues that the NCAA tackles, there was a split in the constituency as to the type of assistance that could be provided. The Big Ten and the PCC were in favor of need-based scholarships whereby students would be awarded on-campus jobs.[1] Southeastern and Southwest conference representatives advocated for scholarships tied to athletic ability.[1] Ultimately, the need-based model was adapted, leading to the establishment in 1948 of what became known as the "Sanity Code."[1]

The Sanity Code covered areas including recruitment, academic standards, and financial aid.[2] In retrospect, its effectiveness appears to have been limited. Despite strict limits on the types of aid available and an attempt to impose minimum academic performance metrics, abuses of the system continued.

As a result, the Sanity Code was repealed at the NCAA convention in 1951, and the athletic grant-in-aid model was adopted in 1957, which was a de facto affirmation of the position of the SEC and Southwest conferences.[2] Through this development, the concept of a "student athlete" emerged, which by necessity dictated the integration of academics into the eligibility process for intercollegiate competition. This ideal has evolved through many iterations to the manifestation that has persisted most recently.

In 1965, the NCAA promoted the "1.6" rule to establish a minimum high school GPA for athletic scholarships, later upgrading it to a 2.0 GPA hurdle in 1973.[1] Proposition 48 was imposed in 1988 to address grade inflation and required a 2.0 average in a core high school curriculum of 11 courses, along with a floor SAT/ACT score of 700/15.[2] In a move to strengthen this protocol, the NCAA adopted the short lived Proposition 42 in 1989 to disqualify partial qualifiers from aid their freshman year; it was summarily repealed in 1990.[1] Proposition 16 was passed in 1992 in an effort to increase graduation rates by imposing a "sliding scale" for standardized test scores and high school grades that remained above a floor of 700 SAT/17 ACT and 2.0, respectively.[2]

Proposition 16 was considered by many to be materially stricter than Proposition 48. It also further ignited the controversy surrounding the potential disparate impact of academic and test score standards on underrepresented groups. The controversy continues to this day, with the NCAA publishing annual data on graduation and academic success, as well as sponsoring surveys on longer-term outcomes among alumni of its athletic programs.

As such, it is apparent that the debate over amateurism certainly is not new. Whether it is need-based grants, on-campus jobs, or scholarships based on athletic ability, the NCAA and its member institutions have sought to keep academics as the focal point of the equation. The efficacy of these measures is debatable, while the intent has been clear.

While the broader universe of college athletics stakeholders has argued over the definition of a "student athlete" and conflated that moniker with a purist definition of amateurism, the tax code makes no mention of the term "student athlete" in the portion of Section 501(c)(3) that addresses athletic competition. Remember that the TRA of 1976 that created the exemption for amateur athletics was predicated on incubating future Olympians and did not contemplate the difference between a student athlete and a non–student athlete. Academics are therefore irrelevant to this specific exemption.

The only prerequisite under Section 501(c)(3) as amended by the TRA of 1976 is that exempt athletic competition be "amateur" in nature. It can be argued further that this concept of an amateur from the U.S. Code does not conform to the strict constructionist definition that has pervaded the debate over amateurism in college sports. Rather, it is a much broader statutory designation that encompasses a wide variety of scenarios.

The Merriam-Webster Dictionary defines an amateur as "one who engages in a pursuit, study, science, or sport as a pastime rather than as a profession."[3] *Pastime* is clearly delineated as being synonymous with the practice of amateurism, whereas amateur is explicitly defined as being exclusive of anything *professional*. By extension, this requires analyzing the definitions of "pastime" and "professional," given their mutually exclusive delegations within the definition of amateur.

A *pastime* is described in the Merriam-Webster Dictionary as "something that amuses and serves to make time pass agreeably."[3] This could apply to a myriad of activities. It also brings up an important point. As is the case in many complexities in the IRC and statutes broadly, it is often easier to explain something less by describing what it *is* and more by making it clear what it is *not*. In the aforementioned definition, an amateur is unequivocally defined as someone who is *not* a *professional*.

Hence, we arrive at the categorization of *nonprofessionalism* to describe the practice of avoiding a clearly delineated violation of amateurism. Moreover, as this chapter embraces the topic of nonprofessionalism, its purpose is to explain this theory rather than define it. Nonetheless, we need to look at one more definition to begin this explanation.

In the same previously cited dictionary, a *professional* is articulated in several different definitions. The only two of these that do not further confuse by reiterating the word *profession* or *professional* are:[3]

1. participating for gain or livelihood in an activity or field of endeavor often engaged in by amateurs; or
2. engaged in by persons receiving a financial return.

Key takeaways from this definition of *professional* are twofold. First, when professional is used as a qualifier (e.g., in the case of a professional golfer), it is often referring to a discipline that is in the default case an amateur pursuit. As sports were originally amateur in nature, this definition offers a strong argument that the benefit of the doubt should be given for anyone describing themselves as a "golfer" or a "football player" that they are most likely not professionals. Secondly, we have a clear demarcation of a professional as one who receives a financial return. More succinctly, this definition could have been further refined by stating that the professional being defined receives financial return *from a particular activity*, versus an open-ended concept of receiving a financial return without specificity about what is generating the return. To illustrate, under this more specific definition, it is clear that a person working as an attorney and being compensated for legal advice, but also playing racquetball in their spare time, can be designated a professional as it regards the law but not in the sport of racquetball.

Hereafter, we will refer to our definition of professional as *one who engages in and receives financial return from a particular activity*. Once again, the purpose of this chapter is not to define nonprofessionalism but rather to explain it. Definitions are by their nature discrete, whereas explanations are continuous. We are shifting the scope of the debate to nonprofessionalism versus professionalism, as it is clear that prior attempts to define this topic from the binary point of view of amateur versus nonamateur have not had continuity with precedent.

Looking back over the history of the industry, it is apparent that amateurism in that myopic sense never really existed. Players have been receiving booster money for a hundred years. More recently, the Supreme Court approved Alston payments, which are stipends of up to $5,980 annually that are paid directly to the athletes from the school.[4] Finally, we now have NIL payments, which are the topic of the next chapter.

Even in the Olympics, the original inspiration for the TRA, the modus operandi has fallen far short of an ideal definition of amateurism. What has existed, and what should continue to exist indefinitely, is a nonprofessional model. This status has been sufficient to preserve exempt status for individual college programs, the conferences, and the NCAA, and there is no reason to believe it could not do so in perpetuity.

To further prove this, we will go through some examples of professional sports and how they are conducted vis-à-vis amateur (nonprofessional) sports, including instances where the two coexist. Professional sports players represent a small minority of athletes, but they receive a disproportionate share of attention. We will examine some examples that should clarify the distinction of a professional and show that most of sporting activity can be classified as nonprofessional.

Golf is a sport characterized by amateurs and professionals who play side by side with one another. Indeed, amateurs are present at many professional golf tournaments, including major championships such as the Masters, the U.S. Open, the PGA Championship, and the Open Championship (British Open). The United States Golf Association (USGA) has specific rules governing amateur status in golf:[5]

Rule 3: Accepting prize money is not allowed (cash prizes up to a maximum of $1,000 may be accepted).

Rule 2: Amateurs may not play in a golf competition as a professional.

Rule 4: Amateurs are prohibited from accepting payment for giving instruction that is not allowed.

Rule 2: Amateurs are not allowed to hold employment (including self-employment) as a golf club or driving range professional.

Rule 2: Amateurs may not hold membership in an association of professional golfers (such as the PGA of America).

While following these guidelines, amateurs may still compete in professional golf tournaments and retain their amateur status, as long as they do not accept prize money above a certain limit. USGA rules allow amateurs to accept financial assistance from individuals and businesses to defray expenses. In addition, amateur golfers can teach or coach at educational institutions, as long as golf instruction comprises less than 50 percent of their duties.[5] Prize limits also only apply to competitions involving "rounds" of golf and are not in force for other types of contests such as longest drive, nearest to the hole, and putting competitions.[5]

Tennis is another sport whereby amateurs play in the same events as professionals. Nonprofessionals can be seen on the courts at bellwether tournaments such as the U.S. Open, Wimbledon, the French Open, and the Australian Open. The United States Tennis Association (USTA) lists receiving prize money from a tournament in excess of expenses for participating as a cause for disqualification from amateur status.[6] Otherwise, amateurs are permitted to play in nearly every USTA tournament, with certain tournaments being available only to amateurs.

Turning to the Olympics, for which the exemption in the TRA was created, we find large swaths of sports that are exclusively amateur in practice. We list the official Olympic sports here to show that most of them do not currently have professional applications. The list is as follows:[7]

Acrobatic Gymnastics	Diving	Skeleton
Alpine Skiing	Equestrian	Ski Jumping
Archery	Fencing	Ski Mountaineering
Artistic Gymnastics	Figure Skating	Snowboard
Artistic Swimming	Flag Football	Speed Skating
Athletics	Freestyle Skiing	Sport Climbing
Badminton	Futsal	Squash
Baseball Softball	Golf	Surfing
Basketball	Handball	Swimming
Basketball 3 × 3	Hockey	Table Tennis
Beach Handball	Ice Hockey	Taekwondo
Beach Volleyball	Judo	Tennis
Biathlon	Karate	Trampoline
Bobsleigh	Lacrosse	Triathlon
Boxing	Luge	Volleyball
Breaking	Marathon Swimming	Water Polo
Canoe Slalom	Modern Pentathlon	Weightlifting
Canoe Sprint	Nordic Combined	Wrestling
Cricket	Rhythmic Gymnastics	
Cross-Country Skiing	Roller Speed Skating	
Curling	Rowing	
Cycling BMX Freesty.	Rugby Sevens	
Cycling BMX Racing	Sailing	
Cycling Mountain Bike	Shooting	
Cycling Road	Short Track Speed Sk.	
Cycling Track	Skateboarding	

Regardless of their lack of widespread professional application, Olympic sports have seen their share of controversy over the concept of amateurism. Originally, from the time the first games were held in Athens in 1896, amateur status was a prerequisite for competition. In fact, U.S. Olympian Jim Thorpe was stripped of his 1912 gold medals in decathlon and pentathlon for having played semiprofessional baseball in college.[8] This in part reflected an aristocratic idealization of competition without compensation that prevailed in certain European countries involved in international competition at the time. Given the fact that, as mentioned in Chapter 3, college sports evolved out of a desire to emulate British athleticism, this likely drove the conception of volunteerism in college athletics.

Over subsequent decades, driven by the desire for commercial success and the ambition of certain regimes to dominate Olympic competition as a nonmilitary Cold War maneuver, the games underwent a metamorphosis away from a pure amateur model. In the 1980s, various Olympic federations began to eliminate amateur requirements.[8] The transition culminated in the 1992 Barcelona Olympics, when the U.S. "Dream Team," led by Michael Jordan and Magic Johnson, decisively earned a gold medal in basketball.[7]

Despite the removal of a formal requirement for amateur status to compete in the Olympics, the athletes are not paid directly for competing. Governing bodies such as the International Olympic Committee (IOC), founded in 1894, provide governance for sporting events dominated by amateurs.[9] To provide more localized oversight, the first U.S. Olympic governing body, the American Olympic Association (AOA), was created in 1921 at the New York Athletic Club.[9] The AOA later became the United States of America Sports Federation in 1940. It then changed its name again to the United States Olympic Association (USOA) after World War II, before being granted a federal charter and tax-exempt status in 1950, coincident with the passage of the Tax Code of 1950.[9] In 1961, amid some revisions to its organization documents, the USOA became the United States Olympic Committee (USOC).[8]

In 1978, Congress passed the Amateur Sports Act, which delegated authority for all Olympic activity in the United States to the USOC.[9] The Act also sought to encourage broader participation in sports, particularly amateur sports. In 1998, the Act was updated and became known as the Ted Stevens Olympic and Amateur Sports Act, named after the long-serving Alaska senator.[9] The USOC ultimately became the United States Olympic & Paralympic Committee (USOPC) in 2019.[9]

The bylaws of the USOPC—as of April 1, 2024—define "amateur athlete" as "any athlete who meets the eligibility standards established by the NGB for the sport in which the athlete competes."[9] NGBs are the National Governing Bodies that coordinate all aspects of their particular sport in the country.[9] There are a total of 50 NGBs in the United States, including 37 for Olympic summer sports, 8 for Olympic winter sports, and 5 for Pan American sports. Overriding all of this, however, is a requirement in the Ted Stevens Act that in order to maintain eligibility to be certified as an NGB, an organization must:[9]

> "not have eligibility criteria related to amateur status or to participation in the Olympic Games, the Paralympic Games, the Pan-American Games, or the Parapan American Games that are more restrictive than those of the appropriate international sports federation."

Through this statement, the Stevens Act—which installed the USOPC as the authority over all Olympic sports in the United States, in turn delegating responsibility for eligibility requirements to the NGBs—essentially cedes control over the determination of amateur status for the Olympic games to the IOC. Ahead of the 2024 Olympic games in Paris, the IOC published its key principles relating to Rule 40, which governs commercial opportunities for Olympic athletes. In its principles, the IOC states, in agreement with an athlete-generated statement entitled Athlete's Rights and Responsibilities, that it likewise:[10]

> "aspires to promote the ability and opportunity of athletes to leverage opportunities to generate income in relation to their sporting career, name and likeness, while recognising the intellectual property or rights, rules of the event and of sports organisations as well as the Olympic Charter."[10]

The publication goes on to state:[10]

> "The Principles are clear: athletes are able to generate income through personal sponsorships and appearing in advertising for those sponsors, and can continue to do so by being involved in well-planned advertising during Paris 2024. In addition, it is hoped that the worldwide exposure provided to athletes participating in Paris 2024 through media coverage, including the IOC's global broadcast arrangements, can help raise their profile for years to come."

In its principles, the IOC also adds some basic restrictions concerning those brands that are Olympic Partners versus non-Olympic Partners that have not negotiated deals directly with the IOC or other Olympic organizations. It notes a prohibition on marketing related to tobacco, alcohol, and prohibited drugs, but it otherwise provides blanket permission for athletes to accept endorsements and to promote commercial products during the Paris Olympics.

Anecdotally, we have seen dozens of Olympians receiving sponsorships and commercial endorsements. Rule 40 had originally placed a moratorium on these during the time the Olympic games were being played, but as is apparent from the IOC's recent publication, this is no longer the case. Before, during, and after the Paris games, Olympic athletes had virtually unfettered access to compensation opportunities related to their participation in the events.

This, however, does not make Olympic athletes professionals. According to the IOC—which is defacto empowered by the Ted Stevens Act, a federal law, to set eligibility standards as they relate to amateurism—Olympians remain amateur athletes. Therefore, they persist as amateur athletes under federal law, and by extension, the tax code.

In this way, to the degree that intercollegiate athletics can mirror the conduct of amateurism as exemplified by international athletic competition in the Olympics, it can remain in the favor of the tax code as it concerns amateur athletics. We can consider the Olympics to be an evolving codification of nonprofessionalism. This is given the fact that the Stevens Act inextricably linked the statutory definition of amateurism, which is what the term "nonprofessionalism" seeks to embody, to that promulgated by the international governing bodies for Olympic competition. Furthermore, this entailment prevails irrespective of whether the creators of the TRA of 1976 contemplated relinquishing such authority to a foreign committee. This is because (1) the Stevens Act postdated the TRA of 1976 and therefore supersedes it; and (2) the original intent of the TRA was to promote Olympic competition, and therefore this interpretation is in line with the spirit as well as the letter of that law.

So, how can college sports remain nonprofessional? As is evident from the examples provided, in those environments where professionals and nonprofessionals cohabitate, it is almost exclusively the case that the athletes are independent contractors. Pure professional environments are characterized by players who are employed by sports franchises or leagues. In these situations, nonprofessionals are necessarily excluded.

Full-time professionals enjoy the benefit of having their costs covered and are guaranteed at least a base salary and typically a certain level of compensation. Conversely, contractors are not guaranteed a profit from their activities after factoring in expenses. In golf, both professionals and nonprofessionals are independent contractors, responsible for covering the costs of equipment, transportation, lodging, and other overhead, such as payment for caddies and swing coaches. The difference is that the former are entitled to receive prize money whereas the latter are not.

Once someone is employed as a full-time athlete, they have clearly crossed the threshold to professionalism. If your title is defined as a spot on the roster of a professional sports team, and you are in an employer–employee relationship with that team or league, you have relinquished any pretense of nonprofessionalism. Independent contractors can be either professionals or nonprofessionals, with the difference often relating to acceptance of payment for participating in an event or prize money for a certain level of performance at a specific contest.

Even after the NCAA settlement, the current situation in college sports can still be considered nonprofessional in the same manner as the Olympics, which is necessary and sufficient to meet the requirement for amateurism under the tax code. Whether it remains that way will depend on the details of the revenue-sharing arrangement. To the extent such revenue distributions are widely dispersed to players and do not relate to participation in or performance at a specific game, then we can conclude that nonprofessionalism stands.

Additional support for the nonprofessional status of college athletes is that they are also full-time students. Previously, it was made clear that status as a student did not have any relevance to the amateur sports exemption. However, to the extent that meeting the requirements for full-time education precludes one from being employed as a professional sports player, it does attain some importance.

Full-time matriculation may help college athletics maintain its exemption under amateurism by proving nonprofessionalism. Moreover, enrollment as a student of the sponsoring institution is critical to the determination that college athletics contributes importantly to the school's primary educational mission. It would be very difficult to argue that college teams staffed with full-time athletes contribute positively to any educational standard. If anything, such an enterprise could be deemed a material distraction to such a purpose. As such, professionalized college athletics would likely be unable to maintain its educational exemption.

Professionalism is therefore anathema to both tax exemptions currently maintained by intercollegiate athletics. Rather than exist independently, these two exemptions actually are highly interrelated. The ideal scenario is a partnership of the two.

Attendance in class supports nonprofessionalism, which is necessary for educational value. The codependence is such that nonprofessionalism is likely the predicate condition—that is, nonprofesionalism could exist without educational value but not vice versa. Nonprofessionalism could likely stand on its own as the single exemption. This would be applicable in a situation where rules have broken down and players who have exhausted their eligibility and/or are no longer enrolled at the school are allowed to compete. In this case, the institution would still be covered under nonprofessionalism.

This is why it is of the utmost importance for college sports to maintain a nonprofessional status. Not only does this endear college sports to the exemption in the tax code for amateur sports, but it is also a key component of retaining educational value and qualifying for exemption as such. A professionalized system in college athletics would forego both exemptions.

Key takeaways from this chapter:

1. The debate over professionalism versus amateurism in college athletics has been going on for the better part of a century, and the 19th century ideal of service without compensation was essentially vacated in the early 1900s.
2. College sports as an industry has clung to an antiquated definition of amateurism based on the concept of a student athlete, academics, and pure volunteerism. It is argued here that the applicable standard should instead be nonprofessionalism, which more closely approximates the view of amateurism taken by the tax code.
3. As an industry, intercollegiate athletics should be able to retain its exemptions for both substantially supporting education and promoting amateur sports to the extent that athletes remain independent contractors and do not enter into an employer–employee relationship with their respective institutions.

NIL

The issue of payment for the use of NIL came on the scene roughly 30 years ago in the 1990s as sports video games enjoyed robust popularity. College athletes whose names, images and/or likenesses were featured in certain games were denied compensation due to NCAA rules that enjoined players from profiting from their respective sports. Some of these players pursued legal actions that drove changes to laws and regulations governing NIL.

In 2014, video game maker EA Sports settled a lawsuit brought by a former UCLA basketball player and a class of plaintiffs agreeing to pay $40 million to roughly 29,000 players whose NILs were featured in its *NCAA March Madness* game.[1] The NCAA was also named in the lawsuit but declined to settle. Instead, the NCAA lost on trial and on appeal and was forced to increase its grant-in-aid limit to the full cost of attendance and permit up to $5,000 per year in additional compensation.[1,2]

This civil action, and others like it, were catalyzed by strict constructionist regulations enforced by the NCAA in a futile attempt to maintain an unrealistic standard of amateurism. It is a basic violation of ethics to utilize something of value owned by another person and refuse to provide renumeration. Any rule that infringes on this ethical principle deserves to be voided.

Nonetheless, under the guidelines promulgated by the NCAA at the time, players could not receive payments for NIL usage. The rules specifically proscribed the practice although schools, conferences, and the NCAA profited from their use. A better policy would have simply been to prohibit the use of athletes' NIL if they could not be paid under NCAA rules. This, however, is not how history unfolded.

In the wake of the EA Sports settlement and NCAA decision, California passed the "Fair Pay to Play Act" in 2019, which immunized college athletes from sanctions by the NCAA or member institutions for NIL earnings.[2] In 2020, Colorado, Florida, Nebraska, New Jersey, and a number of other states followed with legislation permitting NIL payments, much of which was scheduled for enactment in 2022 and 2023. Also in 2020, the NAIA, a competitor to the NCAA that regulates college athletics at 252 typically smaller member schools, enacted regulations allowing NIL compensation for student athletes.[2]

The year 2021 saw a Supreme Court decision in the case of *NCAA v. Alston*, whereby the NCAA was denied an appeal of its antitrust lawsuit.[2] This decision paved the way for what are now known as "Alston Awards" involving direct payments to athletes from schools for academic achievements, and it permitted the NCAA to cap these grants at $5,980 annually.[3] It further drove the NCAA to officially change its stance on monetary rewards for the use of NIL.

On July 1, 2021, the NCAA adopted its Interim NIL Policy.[4] The policy provides the following guidance:[4]

- Individuals can engage in NIL activities that are consistent with the law of the state where the school is located. Colleges and universities may be a resource for state law questions.
- College athletes who attend a school in a state without an NIL law can engage in this type of activity without violating NCAA rules related to NIL.
- Individuals can use a professional services provider for NIL activities.
- Student athletes should report NIL activities consistent with state law or school and conference requirements to their school.

Then NCAA President Mark Emmert further qualified why this is an "interim" policy:[4]

> "With the variety of state laws adopted across the country, we will continue to work with Congress to develop a solution that will provide clarity on a national level. The current environment—both legal and legislative—prevents us from providing a more permanent solution and the level of detail student-athletes deserve."

In its announcement, the NCAA stated that the Interim NIL Policy did not constitute "pay for play" and that NIL could not be used to encourage recruits to attend a particular school.

In a subsequent publication, entitled "Interim Name Image and Likeness Policy Guidance Regarding Third Party Involvement," the NCAA provided updated restrictions on NIL. Specifically referenced in the publication are boosters. Therein, the NCAA defines a "booster" as:[4]

> "...an individual, independent agency, corporate entity (e.g., apparel or equipment manufacturer) or other organization who is known (or who should have been known) by a member of the institution's executive or athletics administration to have participated in or to be a member of an agency or organization promoting an institution's intercollegiate athletics program or to assist or to have assisted in providing benefits to enrolled student-athletes or their family members."

The NCAA underscored rules relating to the conduct of boosters. Specifically, the NCAA reiterates that boosters are precluded from engaging in recruiting activities, including any recruiting related conversations, on behalf of an institution. Additionally, the NCAA's rules forbid boosters from providing benefits to prospective student athletes (PSAs) and disallow any involvement by institutional personnel in the provision of benefits to a PSA. Further, the NCAA states that its existing prohibitions related to pay-for-play have not been altered regarding the Interim NIL Policy.[4]

Additional bullet points highlighted in this NCAA directive include:[4]

- An NIL agreement between a PSA and a booster/NIL entity may **not** be guaranteed or promised contingent on initial or continuing enrollment at a particular institution.
- Institutional coaches and staff may **not** organize, facilitate or arrange a meeting between a booster/NIL entity and a PSA.
- Institutional coaches and staff may **not** communicate directly with a PSA on behalf of a booster/NIL entity.
- *NIL agreements **must** be based on an independent, case-by-case basis of the value that each athlete brings to an NIL agreement as opposed* to providing compensation or incentives for enrollment decisions (e.g., signing a letter of intent or transferring), athletic performance (e.g., points scored, minutes played, winning a contest), achievement (e.g., starting position, award winner) or membership on a team.

Applicable NCAA legislation referred to includes:[4]

- NCAA Bylaw 11.1.13—Athletics department staff members are prohibited from representing a PSA or enrolled student-athlete (SA) in marketing their athletics ability or reputation.
- NCAA Bylaw 13.10—Publicity—Before a PSA signs a National Letter of Intent (NLI) or written offer of admission and/or financial aid or before the institution receives a financial deposit, an institution may comment publicly only to the extent of confirming its recruitment of the PSA.

From the aforementioned guidance, it is clearly the NCAA's intent to divorce host institutions from the process of NIL arrangements and unequivocally to proscribe the use of NIL in the recruiting equation. Nonetheless, in the absence of a permanent policy, institutions and states have moved with alacrity to embrace NIL. Certain movements have expanded the role of schools in facilitating NIL revenue for their players.

In April of 2024, Virginia Governor Glenn Youngkin signed a bill into law that would allow colleges and universities in the state, including the flagship UVA, to participate principally in NIL arrangements including paying student athletes NIL compensation directly.[5] The sponsors of the bill cited similar legislative action in Missouri, New York, Oklahoma, and Texas that put Virginia institutions at a competitive disadvantage.[5]

Oklahoma's governor Kevin Stitt approved a law that would ensure that NIL revenue would not interfere with an athlete's grant-in-aid and that athletic organizations and conferences could not penalize student athletes for receiving NIL compensation. The law goes on to outline that student athletes are *not* considered employees of their respective institutions.[6] Texas in particular passed an aggressive NIL bill that allows boosters to fund NIL arrangements.[7] Missouri further successfully spearheaded NIL legislation that is considered one of the most progressive regimes in the country in that it allows high school students who sign a National Letter of Intent (NOLI) to earn NIL money.[8]

Along with legislation, schools have moved to set up captive NIL vehicles. UVA's NIL collective is known as *Cav Futures*. This organization leverages contributions from donors and support from UVA and its athletics department to facilitate a market in NIL for Virginia athletes. Other similar entities include *Yea Alabama* at the University of Alabama, the *Classic City Collective* at the University of Georgia, and *The Varsity Collective* at the University of Wisconsin. Texas alone has 12 separate NIL collectives in its state related to its various higher education establishments.

As this book goes to print, 32 states have passed some form of NIL legislation.[9] In addition, nearly all of the member institutions of the Power 5 conferences have seeded at least one NIL collective. These numbers are expected to continue to increase.

States That Have Passed NIL Legislation	
Arizona	New Jersey
Arkansas	New Mexico
California	New York
Colorado	North Carolina
Connecticut	Ohio
Delaware	Oklahoma
Florida	Oregon
Georgia	Pennsylvania
Illinois	South Carolina
Indiana	Tennessee

Iowa	Mississippi
Kansas	Missouri
Kentucky	Montana
Louisiana	Nebraska
Maine	Nevada
Maryland	Tennessee
Michigan	Texas
Minnesota	Virginia

A sample of NIL collectives and their respective institutions include:[10]

Collective	Institution	Collective	Institution
Yea Alabama	University of Alabama	Empower the Nest	Illinois State
Tigma	Appalchin State	Hoosiers Connect	Indiana University
Sun Angel	Arizona State	The Swarm Collective	University of Iowa
Arizona Assist Club	University of Arizona	We Will Collective	Iowa State
Arkansas Edge	University of Arkansas	Legends of Kansas	University of Kansas
On to Victory	Auburn University	The Wildcats' Den	Kansas State
Feed the Bird Foundation	Ball State	Club Blue	University of Kentucky
GXG	Baylor University	502 Circle	Louisville
The Horseshoe Collective	Boise State	Boyou Traditions	LSU
Friends of the Heights	Boston College	The Thunder Trust	Marshall
The Ziggy Collective	Bowling Green University	Hard Shell Collective	University of Maryland
Home of the Brave	Bradley University	Bring Back the U	Miami University
All Good Dawgs	Bryant University	Spartan Dawg 4 Life	Michigan State
CougConnect	BYU	Champions Circle	University of Michigan
California Legends	University of California	Pack of Wolves	NC State

Collective	Institution	Collective	Institution
110 Society	Clemson	1890 Nebraska	University of Nebraska
The Teal Collective	Coastal Carolina	Heels4Life	University of North Carolina
5430 Alliance	University of Colorado	Irish United	Notre Dame
The Green & Gold Guard	Colorado State	Cohesion Foundation	Ohio State
Bleeding Blue for Good	University of Connecticut	Crimson & Cream	University of Oklahoma
Pride of Omaha	Creighton	Pokes with a Purpose	Oklahoma State
Exit 30 Collective	Davidson	The Grove Collective	Ole Miss
Durham Devils Club	Duke	Ducks Rising	University of Oregon
Florida Victorious	University of Florida	Happy Valley United	Penn State
Rising Spear	Florida State	Boilermaker Alliance	Purdue
Bulldog Bread	Fresno State	Texas One	University of Texas
Friends of George	George Washington	Texas Aggies United	Texas A&M

These initiatives put the states and the institutions at odds with the NCAA's attempts to disaggregate NIL from school athletics departments and administrations. It is therefore apparent that a federal solution is necessary to prevent the situation from devolving into further chaos. Chaos is very often the incubator of truly bad ideas, and there are enough of those floating around already. We delve into this further in a later chapter.

Other than the conflict between the NCAA, its member institutions, and the states, NIL has been a predominantly positive development for the industry. While it may seem to the contrary, NIL is actually beneficial from a tax perspective. This is due to numerous reasons.

First, NIL compensation arrangements provide a taxable source of revenue for the Treasury department. Unlike media, attendance, and other revenue that is shielded by college athletics' dual exemptions, money paid to athletes for use of their

NIL is fully taxable as ordinary income. In this way, the U.S. taxpayer benefits from the success of college sports, and the argument that the average citizen is somehow being cheated by a highly profitable and greedy business is precluded.

Second, NIL revenue reduces the dependence of student athletes on their host institution. This has important implications for the labor issue that will be discussed in Chapter 9. Suffice it to say, it is highly positive contributor to the argument against professionalization.

Most importantly, NIL is extremely beneficial to the student athletes themselves. Lucrative NIL arrangements provide athletes with compensation while in school and thus allow them to more thoroughly weigh their options. Whereas under the previous regime players would look to go professional as soon as possible, the permission of NIL has actually mitigated adverse trends in college sports such as one-and-done.

It does make sense that the NCAA would not want schools directly involved in the provision of NIL opportunities. This is, again, related to the labor issue to be evaluated in Chapter 9. However, even if schools are themselves involved in creating and paying for NIL arrangements, it does not professionalize college athletics.

This is due to dichotomy of being paid for use of one's NIL as separate and distinct from being paid to play a sport. NIL essentially professionalizes players as models and spokespersons, not as athletes. As such, nonprofessionalism can be maintained with NIL even if directly coordinated or funded by educational institutions.

Returning to our example of the Olympics, we see a wholesale endorsement of NIL as furthering the mission of international competition. The IOC itself, through its own Olympic Broadcasting Services (OBS) organization, is actively seeking to promote NIL opportunities, stating that:[11]

> "...it is hoped that worldwide exposure provided to athletes participating in Paris 2024 through media coverage, including the IOC's global broadcasting arrangements, can help raise their profile for years to come."

The OBS does state, "Our coverage is neutral, favoring no particular country or athlete, and includes sports competitions as well as the Opening and Closing Ceremonies."[12]

While NIL collectives are still new, they will likely benefit from some guidance on standards to maintain going forward. This is why a national consensus in the form of federal legislation is so important at this juncture in time. NIL can and will be a highly productive form of commercial revenue for college athletes, and its success need not diminish nonprofessionalism in intercollegiate athletics.

Another important development to highlight is that on May 23, 2023, a memorandum from the Office of the Chief Counsel of the IRS addressed the tax-exempt status of NIL collectives under Section 501(c)(3). Its conclusion was straightforward:[13]

> "An organization that develops paid NIL opportunities for student-athletes will, in many cases, be operating for a substantial nonexempt purpose—serving the private interests of student-athletes—which is more than incidental to any exempt purpose furthered by the activity."

While this memo cannot be cited as precedent, it should dissuade organizers of these collectives from exploiting them as tax-exempt charities. There is very little basis that these arrangements contribute importantly to the educational mission of the schools or to the promotion of nonprofessional sports. This does not make them catalysts for the professionalization of intercollegiate sports; it just means that the collectives themselves are not exempt.

Another important takeaway from the memo is it states unequivocally, "Student-athletes are not themselves a recognized charitable class."[13] This is supportive of previous conclusions made herein that underscored the fact that the phrase *student athlete* does not appear in Section 501(c)(3) of the tax code. It goes on to state, "While the Service has previously recognized as charitable certain organizations whose activities benefitted student-athletes, the rulings were based on the determination that the activities advanced education."[13]

This guidance is congruent to the conclusions of this book. It is not the athletes themselves that further the exempt purpose, but rather it is the sports that contribute importantly to the educational purpose of the schools—and, through their existence and success, promote nonprofessional athletics. As noted in the memo, there is IRS case precedent for the former conclusion, and this tome argues that there is a strong logical case for the latter as well. From this point of view, the activities of the student athletes as individuals are somewhat irrelevant to the exemption afforded to the sports they play.

Put another way, college athletes can benefit from NIL deals, whether arranged or paid for by third parties or the schools themselves, without impacting the tax-exempt status of intercollegiate athletics broadly. As long as the sports are organized in a nonprofessional manner and contribute importantly to the educational mission of the college or university, they will retain their exemption. NIL should therefore not be viewed as a threat to the persistence of college athletics in its current manifestation.

To the contrary, it appears that NIL has drawn interest from outside sources of capital whose contributions may be able to defray the additional expense associated with the settlement. These sources are more investors than contributors and do not seek tax benefits in the same manner as regular way charitable donors. As such, the

NIL collectives could make desirable mechanisms to participate in intercollegiate athletics.

A recent article in *The Wall Street Journal* discussed the burgeoning interest among private equity firms in investing in college sports. Unlike typical private equity deals, this would not involve a control acquisition of a team but rather an investment in intangibles such as intellectual capital and NIL.[14] The article cites a new firm, Collegiate Athletic Solutions (CAS), which plans to partner with college and universities with $50 million to $200 million investments.[14] In turn, CAS will seek to enhance the revenue-generating capabilities of school athletic departments.[14]

Another unforeseen benefit of NIL has been its impact on women's sports. Caitlin Clarke and Livvy Dunne from Indiana University and LSU, respectively, have made great strides in drawing attention to their sports. By using NIL, they have been able to further reach diverse audiences and demographics that would have been elusive under the old regime.

Key takeaways from this chapter include:

1. Permission for players to be compensated for NIL has created friction between the NCAA, its member institutions, and state legislatures as to what guidelines should be established.
2. Despite appearances to the contrary, NIL is actually positive from a tax perspective in that it generates taxable income and creates distinct financial independence of athletes from their host school.
3. Federal legislation will be required to set universal standards for the use of NIL compensation arrangements.

NCAA Settlement

One negative impact of the change in policy regarding NIL is that it opened up a Pandora's Box of litigation related to the prior position. Numerous aggrieved parties have come forward seeking compensation for NIL they would have earned had the NCAA's rule change been applied retroactively. The size and number of these complaints ultimately led to the watershed settlement that was announced in May 2024 and that will be discussed in this chapter.

Topping the headlines among these actions is the case of *House v. the NCAA* and the Power 5 conferences. Brought by Grant House, an Arizona State swimmer, and Sedona Prince, citing a putative class of damaged parties, the suit was filed in the U.S. District Court of Northern California in June of 2020, approximately one year prior to the Interim NIL Policy promulgated by the NCAA.[1] The suit alleges antitrust violations and seeks compensation for foregone revenues from the use of the plaintiffs' NIL.[2]

In the introduction to the document, the House suit describes the Zion Williamson sneaker explosion incident as an anecdote for the commercialization of college sports.[1] The action's claims include the NCAA's unlawful regulation of a commercial market in violation of the Sherman Antitrust Act. Further, it states damages beyond a pecuniary nature in that the NCAA's rules deprived plaintiffs' access to key educational pursuits that would have allowed them to develop their brand.[1]

February 2024 saw the Commonwealth of Virginia and the State of Tennessee file suit against the NCAA, challenging its NIL regulations. Plaintiffs are bringing the action *parens patriae* on behalf of their student athlete constituents that they claim have been damaged by the NCAA's actions.[3] It seeks an injunction preventing the NCAA from enforcing its rules against using NIL as an incentive to garner athletic recruits.[3]

The Virginia and Tennessee filing specifically relates to the NIL collectives that have been established at schools nationwide. Based on updated guidance provided by the NCAA that postdated its Interim NIL Policy, these entities are classified as boosters and are therefore enjoined from participating in the recruiting process for fresh athletic talent.[3] The temporary restraining order sought by the complaint would halt the NCAA's enforcement of this recruitment ban.[3]

Not long after Virginia and Tennessee filed, a federal judge granted their request for a preliminary injunction against the NCAA. The decision represented the latest setback in a long string of defeats for the NCAA in court. The restraining order is preliminary, however, and the NCAA is expected to appeal.[4]

Yet another antitrust civil complaint filed in the Northern District of California is being litigated by the same attorneys in the House case as well as the successful Alston case that led to the amended NIL rules. This one alleges that the NCAA and the Power 5 conferences conspired to fix athlete compensation in contravention of antitrust statutes.[5] The named plaintiffs in this case are a Duke football player, a TCU basketball player, and a Stanford soccer player.

A similar case was also brought in Colorado by former football player Alex Fontenot.[6] The action was filed in November 2023 and, in line with the other actions, alleges antitrust violations. In the introduction to the complaint, a Notre Dame versus Ohio State football game is showcased, and the substantial amount of television revenue generated by college football is highlighted, along with the fact that college athletes have historically been prohibited from a sharing in these profits. A particularly poignant point is made in the filing when it cites statistics revealing the fact that most college athletes do not ultimately become paid professionals and, as such, will not have future opportunities to earn renumeration for their talents.[6]

Hubbard v. NCAA was filed in April 2023, again in the Northern District of California. The suit seeks damages from the NCAA's grant-in-aid cap that followed the successful Alston litigation but was ultimately declared unlawful by the courts.[7] In particular, the claims relate to academic achievement awards that were unlawfully capped by the NCAA. Plaintiffs in this case include a former Oklahoma State football player and a former Oregon and Auburn track and field athlete.

More recently, in March of 2024, UNC tennis player Reese Brantmeier filed a class action lawsuit against the NCAA, alleging prize money fixing.[8] This action is unique in that it relates to "nonrevenue" sports. Specifically, the suit seeks damages for restrictions on prize money offered by non-NCAA competitions—such as those hosted by the USTA—that prevent them from exceeding "actual and necessary expenses."

In another very recent example of an NIL derived action, on June 11, 2024, members of the 1983 North Carolina State men's championship basketball team, dubbed the "Cardiac Pack," filed suit against the NCAA for NIL monies. The team had won nine games in overtime by a single point and made it to the national championship, where they earned the title via a single point made in the last seconds of the game.[9] Plaintiffs argued that the NCAA has used their NIL for over 40 years without paying due compensation and without the consent of the players. The complaint asserted that their NIL had been used in the March Madness tournament and was viewable online with commercial royalties paid to the NCAA but not to any of the athletes featured in the video.[9]

Antitrust allegations are not limited to compensation. In December 2023, Colorado, Illinois, New York, North Carolina, Ohio, Tennessee, and West Virginia filed suit challenging the NCAA's transfer rules.[1] In January 2024, the action was joined by the United States Justice Department (DOJ) after the federal court in the Northern District of West Virginia granted a temporary injunction.[10] An amended complaint was submitted on January 18, which included the U.S. government as well as the District of Columbia and the states of Minnesota and Mississippi.[10]

In this unique dispute, the various states and the DOJ are contesting the NCAA's rule against multiple transfers.[11] Specifically, Bylaw 14.5.5.1 "Transfer Eligibility Rule" imposes a one-year delay in the eligibility of certain college athletes transferring between NCAA member institutions.[12] The complaint alleges that this restriction "unfairly restrains the ability of these college athletes to engage in the market for their labor as NCAA Division I college athletes."[11]

Under the NCAA's rules, an athlete is required to be in "academic residency" for one year following a transfer between institutions before regaining eligibility to compete. This "redshirt" year does not count against a player's total eligibility. The requirement is waived for an initial transfer, and there is a process for seeking exceptions. Often, the departure of a coach has been considered a valid reason for a transfer, and athletes have been excepted from the one-year waiting period for this. Nonetheless, the rule remains in place for subsequent transfers.

A large scandal relating to this rule unfolded at St. Bonaventure in 2003. The incident stemmed from the prior year, when the Bonnies' head coach Jan van Breda Kolff recruited Jamil Terrell to play on the men's basketball team.[12] Terrell was a transfer from Coastal Georgia Community College, where he had completed a welding certificate and not the requisite associate's degree for a penalty-free transfer. Terrell's competing in the 2002–2003 season led to the termination of van Breda Kolff and the dismissal of athletic director Gothard Lane and university President Robert Wickenheiser.[12] The NCAA sanctioned Bonaventure with a one-year postseason ban and a three-year probation period. The NCAA also vacated six Atlantic 10 wins and canceled three scholarships. Subsequently, the Atlantic 10 voted the school out of the conference.[12] In the wake of the scandal, chairman of the board of trustees Bill Swan, who was also CEO of a community bank in upstate New York, committed suicide.

More recently, a substantial uproar occurred over the NCAA's designation of a star UNC-Chapel Hill football player as a double transfer. In the 2023 season, wide receiver Devontez "Tez" Walker was ruled ineligible to play during the season by the NCAA, which claimed that Walker had transferred twice as an undergraduate although he had only played football for one prior school.[13] The determination led to some contentious back-and-forth conversation between UNC and the NCAA, including a statement from UNC-Chapel Hill football head coach Mack Brown of, "Shame on you, NCAA. SHAME ON YOU!" Ultimately, the NCAA reversed its decision, citing "new information" received from UNC-Chapel Hill, and Walker was given a waiver to play.[13]

Previously, transfers between member institutions were broadly disallowed and subject to a one-year waiting period for eligibility, even on a first iteration. However, in 2018, the NCAA created the transfer portal, which provides for a time period during which players can declare a transfer; this is typically a two-week period near the end of the season. Players can declare for the transfer portal, which provides the opportunity for coaches and athletics department personnel from other institutions to view athletes interested in transferring and make offers of admission and scholarships. The transfer portal's beginning also coincided with new rules that allowed for student athletes to be immediately eligible to compete after their first transfer.[12]

Very recently, retiring coaches—including hall of famers such as Mike Krzyzewski from Duke and Roy Williams from UNC-Chapel Hill—have blamed the transfer portal for fundamentally changing the coaching experience. It makes sense that coaches would prefer to be able to manage their rosters without the uncertainty created by the ability of students to transfer. However, it is apparent from the legal complaints filed by member institutions and their host states that there is a desire for more mobility within the intercollegiate athletics system.

On April 17, 2024, the Division I Council of the NCAA approved changes to its rules to allow transferring student athletes to be immediately eligible for competition, regardless of the number of times they transfer, provided that they meet certain academic requirements.[12] In particular, athletes will be required to be academically eligible and in good standing at their original institution. The NCAA is also considering the development of a "graduation passport" to track an athlete's academic progress across multiple institutions.[12]

Even as the NCAA moved to mollify complaints over transfer eligibility, the number of legal challenges mounted. Indeed, as 2024 began, the NCAA was facing an unprecedent number of civil actions and complaints. Its track record in court, going all the way back to the original antitrust suit in the 1980s, has also been abysmally poor. With certain class actions seeking billions of dollars in restitution, the cost of failure would be extremely high.

In addition to antitrust claims and the transfer eligibility disputes, the NCAA has also faced what are essentially a handful of labor disputes. These petitions differ from the cacophony of antitrust allegations in that they make the claim that student athletes are essentially employees of the colleges and universities that they play for. This is the topic of the next chapter, but suffice it to say for now that these assertions are categorically rejected by both the NCAA and its member institutions.

If that was not enough, the NCAA is facing blowback from its stance on social issues. In March of 2024, 16 female athletes—representing sports that included swimming, volleyball, and track—filed a complaint in the Northern District of Georgia against the NCAA and other parties. This complaint alleged violation of the plaintiffs' Title IX rights due to the inclusion of transgender women in female athletics.[14] The complaint referenced the 2021–2022 women's swimming season, which captured headlines for the dominance of Lia Thomas, a transgender swimmer from the University of Pennsylvania.[14] Complainants are seeking redress for a violation of their civil rights under federal law.

This was the situation confronting the NCAA in May 2024. While the court dates for many of the actions were still at least a year away, the NCAA was staring down the barrel of potentially tens of billions of dollars of outflows related to antitrust claims. Having yet to prevail in any judiciary setting against such claimants in the past, the NCAA came to the decision to enter into the landmark settlement that was announced that month.

On May 23, 2024, the NCAA announced jointly with the Big Ten, SEC, Pac-12, Big 12, and ACC—along with plaintiff attorneys Hagens Berman and Winston & Strawn LLP—a watershed settlement agreement.[15] The agreement diffuses three of the aforementioned lawsuits—*House v. NCAA, Hubbard v. NCAA,* and *Carter v. NCAA*—that alleged anticompetitive behavior through imposing limits on athlete compensation.[15] The concessions provide for monetary compensation, as well as changes to regulations going forward.

As part of the deal, the agreeing parties will pay more than $2.75 billion in renumeration to student athletes who were class members in the suits. This is a fraction of the potential liability the NCAA and the conferences had faced if they had pursued the matter to trial and lost. Given the NCAA's track record defending antitrust actions, this may not have been the worst course of action.

In addition to monetary consideration, the NCAA and the Power 5 have agreed to update their regulations to allow athletes to be paid directly from their respective institutions.[15] During the first year of effectiveness, each college and university will be permitted to share up to 22 percent of the average Power 5 school revenue intake.[15] This contemplated revenue share would be on top of other forms of compensation, including scholarships, benefits, and third-party NIL arrangements.[15] Any Division I athlete can participate in these payments; it is not limited to revenue sports.[15]

This arrangement also stipulates the end of NCAA scholarship caps.[15] Previously, teams were limited as to the number of scholarships they could offer, and the caps differed among sports. The NCAA had already agreed in a prior settlement that scholarships could cover the complete cost of attendance.

Not covered by this settlement is the *Fontenot v. NCAA* suit. This case is being litigated by different plaintiffs' counsel, and its jurisdiction is in Colorado. The other three were all in the Northern District of California. Further, the settlement is not final. It also does not preclude future actions on the NCAA by litigants who are not a party to this settlement.

The settlement also does not address the prize money issue raised by *Brantmeier v. NCAA*. That action is being brought in North Carolina by two plaintiff firms that are not involved in any of the other discussed cases. Unlike *House, Hubbard*, and *Carter*, it is not as closely related to NIL.

Further issues that remain include the states' attorneys general challenges to recruitment rules governing boosters and NIL collectives. It is not apparent from the settlement as to what role these intermediaries will play in the revenue-sharing arrangement posited by the NCAA's settlement.[16] While long on promises of milestone change, the NCAA's joint statement was short on detail.

The NCAA's announcement also exposes some peripheral concerns related to college sports and higher education in general. First and foremost, among these is Title IX. Additionally, there are eligibility issues related to student athletes who are not U.S. citizens.

As federal law, Title IX prohibits discrimination in federally funded institutions on the basis of sex. As even fully private schools receive some form of federal funds in the form of student aid and/or research grants, nearly every member institution in the NCAA is required to comply with Title IX. As previously discussed, Title IX expanded the number athletic programs offered by colleges and universities to accommodate more women's sports. Similarly, a post-settlement environment that disproportionately benefits men's sports or is unduly detrimental to women's teams will likely run afoul of Title IX.[16]

On immigration, to the extent that certain student athletes who are covered under the settlement—or who will be eligible for revenue share going forward—are non-U.S. citizens, this could affect their ability to participate in these benefits.[16] As college athletics has moved forward to procure additional financial upside for student athletes, there has been some neglect of this issue. It is also not something that the NCAA can unilaterally dispense with in the way that it can override rules and regulations that it had previously established.

The agreement also does not address the labor issue. This remains probably the largest issue outstanding for the NCAA. Due to its complexity and gravity, the entire next chapter is devoted to it. Nothing, however, in what has been officially announced or even theorized about the settlement makes any direct reference to it.

For all the fanfare, the settlement is not really as earth-shattering as it sounds. It provides for some $2.7 billion in damages to be split among the NCAA and the Power 5 conferences and paid out over a period of roughly 10 years. This is a large sum, but it is not likely going to bankrupt any of these entities. In fact, it would not be surprising, given the popularity of college sports, if the various parties simply pass the cost on to the consumer the next time their media rights come up for renewal by advocating for a higher price given the cost of litigation. It will simply be another driver of the expense of content, which has already been steadily increasing.

In addition, the NCAA is backing off its old age proscription against direct compensation by its member institutions to student athletes. However, this was already in the cards given the laws passed by states like Virginia, Tennessee, and others that specifically allowed schools and boosters to directly compensate players through NIL arrangements. The revenue share offered in the settlement is optional to the schools, and to the extent used will likely be just another source of NIL funds. Given the plethora of capital flowing into the industry to facilitate NIL, the member schools are essentially getting in line to be added to the list of investors in a burgeoning trade.

While the settlement is hailed as the "end of amateurism," it has been shown herein that amateurism never really existed in the unadulterated sense in which the NCAA, and other followers of the drama of intercollegiate athletics, saw it. It does not make college athletes professionals, and, as such, we can expect nonprofessionalism to prevail even after the settlement is in effect. This will allow the NCAA and the conferences to maintain their exemptions under the tax code.

With the lack of detail in the joint statement made by the NCAA, the conferences, and the plaintiffs' attorneys, it is hard to speculate what revenue share will ultimately look like. Given the need to comply with Title IX, however, it will most likely take the form of a broad-based dividend to college athletes across both men and women's sports without substantial regard to their relative ability to generate revenue. Expect it to be packaged as an NIL contribution with the potential to involve certain NIL collectives made pariahs by the NCAA but legislated into legitimacy by the various states. While the sums may be large in aggregate, they will not represent a windfall for any specific individual. This is a good thing.

Star athletes will remain capable of seeking and achieving lucrative NIL deals leveraging outside capital, some of which may be facilitated by "booster" NIL collectives. This will not professionalize college sports. At the end of the day, the students are earning this compensation for their NIL much in the same way as models and movie stars are paid—not for their actual participation or level of play in athletics. Let's just hope things stop there.

Key takeaways from this chapter:

1. Following the decision to permit student athletes to profit from their NIL, the NCAA has been beset by legal actions seeking recompense for past NIL usage.
2. In addition to NIL suits, the NCAA also faces suits over prize money fixing and player transfers.
3. While the NCAA announcement of a settlement seeks to resolve several of the federal antitrust lawsuits, it does not address all of the pending legal action. In particular, left open is the labor issue that will be discussed in Chapter 9.

The Labor Issue

In addition to the civil matters discussed in the prior chapter, the NCAA is facing a handful of labor disputes related to the question of whether college athletes are employees of their respective host institutions. The NCAA has argued fervently that student athletes are not employees—and for good reason. An employer–employee relationship between the schools and the athletes would fully professionalize college sports, blow their tax exemption, and lead to expenses substantially greater than those contemplated by the recent NCAA settlement.

One of the most notable labor complications faced by college athletics has been a recent attempt by Dartmouth College basketball players to unionize. On March 5, 2024, the men's basketball team at Dartmouth voted 13 to 2 to be represented by the Service Employees International Union Local 560, which encompasses a number of health-care, public sector, and property services workers including many at Dartmouth.[1] Dartmouth College has refused to recognize the union and has stated unequivocally that it will not engage in collective bargaining with the putative organization.[2] This dispute was seemingly catalyzed by a regional office of the National Labor Relations Board (NLRB) which greenlighted the Dartmouth basketball team's classification as employees, thereby allowing them to unionize.[2] Dartmouth is seeking a review by the full NLRB, which is likely the opening salvo in a protracted legal battle that could end up in federal court.

A similar case is being heard in California, where the general counsel of the NLRB has filed a complaint against USC, the Pac-12 conference, and the NCAA, seeking to enjoin them from misclassifying players as student athletes and rather to categorize them as employees.[3] As employees, college athletes would be able to form unions and engage in collective bargaining with their theorized employers. The case is currently pending.

These two actions are reminiscent of a 2015 petition by the Northwestern University football team to unionize. In this case, similar to the Dartmouth situation, a regional director of the NLRB agreed that players receiving grant-in-aid were employees of the university.[4] Here, upon review of the full NLRB, they declined to assert jurisdiction in the matter.[4] This does not put the matter to rest, however, as described in the text of the August 17, 2015 decision:[4]

> "We conclude that asserting jurisdiction in this case would not serve to promote stability in labor relations. Our decision today is limited to the grant-in-aid scholarship football players covered by the petition in this particular case; whether we might assert jurisdiction in another case involving grant-in-aid scholarship football players (or other types of scholarship athletes) is a question we need not and do not address at this time."

The NLRB did note that it was operating in a vacuum of legislative guidance in declining to impose authority in the Northwestern petition. Specifically, it stated, "... we address this case in the absence of explicit congressional direction regarding whether the Board should exercise jurisdiction."[4] In the absence of such federal legislation, it is hard to foresee what future NLRB decisions on this issue could look like.

At the crux of this debate is whether college athletes are employees of the characteristics of NFL football players and NBA basketball players or rather independent contractors in the manner of PGA golfers and USTA tennis players. As previously discussed, the former are made up exclusively of professionals, whereby the latter can include professionals as well as nonprofessionals. In order to maintain nonprofessionalism, therefore, it is important for college athletes to continue to be regarded as independent contractors.

IRS guidelines on the distinction between employees and contractors are as such:[5]

> "The general rule is that an individual is an independent contractor if the payer has the right to control or direct only the result of the work and not what will be done and how it will be done."

The IRS does state that the distinction "depends on the facts in each case," but otherwise its description of the independent contractor versus employee categorization is fairly direct. From the perspective of the IRS, this has relevance to the extent that independent contractors are subject to self-employment tax. Nonetheless, it is a useful rule of thumb for this discussion, especially as it comes from the federal agency that will ultimately have significant weight in determining the exempt status of college athletics.

The NLRB derives its authority from the National Labor Relations Act (NLRA), also known as the Wagner Act, that was signed by President Franklin Roosevelt in 1935.[6] The Act guaranteed employees "the right to self-organization, to form, join, or assist labor organizations, to bargain collectively through representatives of their own choosing, and to engage in concerted activities for the purpose of collective bargaining or other mutual aid and protection."[6] It created the NLRB to mediate labor disputes, guarantee democratic union elections, and sanction abusive practices by companies in the private sector.[6]

Unlike the IRS, the NLRB's definition of an independent contractor is significantly more complicated. In fact, the NLRB recently adopted new regulations that would further expand the employee designation vis-à-vis that of an independent contractor. Under these new guidelines, millions of workers previously regarded as contractors are expected to be reclassified as full-time employees.[7] The new regulations, which took effect on March 11, 2024, are actually a retrogressive measure to return to prior standards established during the Obama administration that provide for a broader definition of an employee.

The new rules provide for a six-factor economic realities test for the Department of Labor (DOL) to determine independent contractor status, emphasizing an equal application. The six factors are as follows:[7]

1. worker's opportunity for profit or loss;
2. investments by the worker and potential employer;
3. degree of permanence of the work relationship;
4. skills and initiative;
5. extent to which work performed is an integral part of the potential employer's business; and
6. nature and degree of control.

On the first of these criteria, there is the concept of opportunity for profit and loss. An NFL player who shows up to play a game is reasonably assured of getting a paycheck, whereby a golfer who competes in a tournament and misses the cut may end up with a loss for the weekend after factoring in expenses.* The former is clearly an employee, whereas the latter is an independent contractor.

Regarding the second economic factor, investments by the worker and potential employer, a similar example is relevant. NBA and NFL players compete wearing jerseys and using equipment provided by their teams. Their training activities are sponsored by their respective franchises. PGA golfers are responsible for the cost of their clothes, clubs, transportation, and caddies. Again, the former are employees whereas the latter are contractors.

Third, the degree of permanence of the work relationship is again a clear differentiator of professional employees versus professional or nonprofessional contractors. Professional sports leagues have guaranteed agreements that cover a specified period of time. Up until they are traded, they are employed by the franchise that drafted or recruited them. Tennis players and golfers do not work for the PGA, USTA, or any specific franchise. They are self-employed.

---

* Not considering guaranteed compensation recently implemented by the PGA.

On the fourth economic criterion—skills and initiative—it used to be that specialized skills would automatically qualify someone as an independent contractor. Under the new guidelines, this is no longer the case. Important now is whether specialized skills are used "in connection with a business-like initiative."[7] This makes sense for independent sports participants in that their specialized skills allow them to qualify for certain events, thereby advancing their business initiatives.

Fifth, in determining an independent contractor versus employee relationship, businesses are supposed to ascertain the extent to which the individual's contributions are critical to the organization's operations and mission.[7] The more indispensable a human resource is to a group, the more likely he or she is to be considered an employee. Those who perform peripheral functions are more easily placed in the contractor bucket.

Finally, nature and degree of control echoes a theme similar to the IRS definition. To the extent that an institution dictates the timing, nature, and location of work to be performed, the likelihood that its workers will be considered employees increases. Flexible workers, such as those who exist in the gig economy, are usually contractors by default.

The distinction is important for many reasons. Most applicable here is that employees in certain states have the right to unionize, whereas independent contractors very rarely do. Employees fall under state minimum wage laws and are often entitled to certain benefits and protections. Independent contractors, by the fact that they are self-employed, usually cannot avail themselves of the entitlements of labor regulations. Additionally, workers classified as employees are further classified into two categories under DOL guidelines: exempt and nonexempt. The former are not entitled to overtime compensation, whereas the latter are.

Very recently, the DOL issued guidance under the Fair Labor Standards Act (FLSA) that would greatly expand the categorization of employees as nonexempt. Exempt status now requires both a salary test as well as a function test to make this determination.[7] Such new guidance is expected to vastly increase the number of employees who are considered nonexempt and therefore entitled to overtime.[7]

The FLSA, passed in 1938, created regulations on minimum wage, overtime pay, recordkeeping, and child labor.[8] Overtime pay is required for nonexempt workers who put in more than 40 hours in a given week. Such overtime pay must be at least one and a half times the employee's regular pay rate.[8]

Under updated FLSA regulations, companies should employ the following test in determining exempt versus nonexempt status:[7]

1. Is the employee paid at least $1,059 per week?
2. Does the employee's pay remain unaffected based on variations in the quantity/quality of work performed?

3. Does the employee perform jobs that could be described as executive, administrative, professional/creative, related to computers, or related to outside sales?
4. Assuming the employee potentially qualifies as exempt, what does a thorough analysis of job duties, which must be performed, determine?

In this test, a "no" answer to any of the first three questions disqualifies a position from exemption. Given the scope of job duties that lie outside of these descriptions, it is likely that a significant number of workers would fail to qualify as exempt under the updated guidelines. Moreover, to the extent college athletics became professionalized by unionization, the players would almost certainly be considered nonexempt and entitled to overtime.

Nonprofits and organized labor have historically had an interesting relationship. Organized labor unions themselves qualify for exemption from taxes, but, unlike higher educational institutions, they are not considered charities (i.e., they cannot solicit tax-deductible donations). Charities and nonprofits traditionally have been hosts to labor unions arranged by their employees in a complementary manner that often furthers the beneficent goals of both groups. Where there is conflict, however, the situation becomes more complicated.

Charitable organizations are generally not considered covered enterprises under the FLSA.[9] In order to be covered under the FLSA, charitable organizations must meet two criteria:[9]

1. They must have an annual dollar volume of sales or businesses done of at least $500,000.
2. They must be a hospital, business providing medical or nursing care for residents, school or preschool, or government agency.

The DOL goes on to state that charitable organizations are only covered under the FLSA if they engage in "ordinary commercial activities." The concept of "ordinary commercial activities" is congruent with IRS guidance on UBTI. In this way, there is a circularity of the relationship between charitable exemption for college athletics and coverage under the FLSA. As charities, college sports should not be covered by the FLSA. However, to the extent that they become professionalized through unionization and the establishment of an employer–employee relationship, they will likely lose their charitable status and thereby become covered by the FLSA. It is a chicken and egg paradox, yet one that can be avoided through common sense legislation.

Beyond college sports, the issue of whether higher educational institutions are covered under the FLSA is a much broader issue and one that has been contentious in recent years. Certain employees of colleges and universities, including some faculty, have argued that the institutions engage in enough commercial activity to be beholden to labor regulations. It is not a question that is going to be answered anytime soon, and it is a wider realm that goes beyond the scope of this book.

Whether certain other classifications of workers at universities can form unions is something that will ultimately be decided by court precedent. The argument for the unionization of college athletes, however, is spurious. This is because categorizing student athletes as full-time employees with entitlement to benefits and overtime is fraught with many logical inconsistencies.

First and foremost of these inconsistencies is that college players cannot simultaneously be full-time workers and full-time students. The IRS defines a full-time student as "a student who is enrolled for the number of hours or courses that the school considers to be full-time attendance."[10] More specifically, the IRS has determined:[10]

> To qualify as a student, the person must be, during some part of each of any five calendar months of the year:
>
> 1. a full-time student at a school that has a regular teaching staff, course of study, and regularly enrolled student body; or
> 2. a student taking a full-time, on-farm training course given by a school described in (1) or by a state, county, or local government agency.
>
> The five calendar months are not required to be consecutive.

Given the fact that a prerequisite of eligibility for participation in intercollegiate athletics is enrollment as a full-time student in compliance with the aforementioned IRS guidelines, this precludes them from realistically being categorized as full-time employees.

The other inconsistency is that based on the previously described guidance from the DOL and NLRB, to the extent that student athletes do receive renumeration, their classification would be that of independent contractors, not direct employees of the institutions. This was true in the environment before the NCAA settlement, and it will also probably be true in what is likely to prevail after the settlement. In both scenarios, most compensation that student athletes are receiving/will receive is in the form of NIL arrangements, with their Alston payments being essentially rendered *de minimis* by the significantly larger NIL opportunity. Under this regime, the athletes would clearly be considered contractors, even under the tightened regulations promulgated by the NLRB.

On the first of the six factors, opportunity for profit or loss, it is clear that the individual student athletes bear the risk–reward aspect of NIL. Athletes can spend time and money marketing themselves to potential NIL providers, but they might ultimately not be successful. Even if an NIL collective facilitates this process, it is still a third party external to the educational institution, even if some of the money is provided by the school.

Secondly, regarding investments by the worker and employer, it is obvious that the student athlete is investing the time and effort to discover potential NIL opportunities. To the extent that monetary investment is provided by collectives or boosters, these parties are nonetheless separate and distinct from the putative employer–employee relationship. No matter who puts up the capital, these investments are driven by the athlete, not by the school.

With the third factor, degree of permanence of the relationship, these NIL arrangements are evanescent in nature. It will likely be the case as the industry develops that student athletes will have multiple NIL partners such that no one group will command significant market power. As such, even if the educational institution itself is an NIL partner with its student athletes, it would be one of several, if not more, and therefore offer no permanence of relationship.

On skills and initiative, the specialized skills of college athletes would normally have qualified them as independent contractors *ipso facto*. Even under the revised guidelines, the prominence of certain athletes that gains them NIL contracts creates a specialization that negates any dependence on the institution in an employer–employee fashion. Therefore, on these criteria, college athletes are clearly independent contractors.

The athletes' NIL activities are in no way integral to the operations of college athletics. In this way, their revenue-generating occupations are peripheral in nature to the crux of the institution's sports initiatives. This argues strongly in favor of them being classified as independent contractors.

On nature and degree of control, college athletes are masters of their own destinies in the NIL space. Educational institutions can influence and even facilitate NIL relationships, but they are not the ultimate deciders of how athletes' NIL is used. In this way, the autonomy given to players in the NIL world categorizes them inextricably as independent contractors and not employees of their respective institutions.

In conclusion for this chapter, therefore, under the current and likely future post-settlement situation, college athletics can avoid professionalization by categorizing players as independent contractors. Attempts to unionize and otherwise classify student athletes as employees are based on indefensible arguments that should be vigorously contested. In this way, nonprofesssionalism can be maintained, and the tax exemptions enjoyed by college sports can be preserved.

Key takeaways from this chapter include:

1. The NCAA and college athletics have been beset by controversial labor claims aiming to unionize student athletes and therefore professionalize the industry.
2. To the extent that college athletes become employees of the institutions they play for, they would likely be entitled to benefits and overtime.
3. Under current and likely future NIL arrangements, college sports participants are most correctly categorized as independent contractors, thereby precluding an employer–employee relationship and any right to unionize.

The Case for Exemption

Tax disputes in the United States can be pursued through numerous channels. Petitioners can seek redress in U.S. Tax Court, a U.S. District Court, or the U.S. Court of Federal Claims. Either the IRS or a taxpayer can initiate a process in these primary trial courts for resolving a tax dispute. The U.S. Courts of Appeals and the Supreme Court of the United States are appellate courts, which review the trial record of lower courts to determine whether the law was appropriately applied.

The most popular of these channels is U.S. Tax Court for the simple reason that it is the only means of recourse that does not require the payment of any disputed tax amounts in advance of the proceedings. The U.S. Tax Court exists only to hear federal tax cases, which are adjudicated by a trial judge who is a tax expert. Taxpayers can represent themselves in trials that are catalyzed by an IRS notice of deficiency. There are no juries in these trials.

Decisions in U.S. Tax Court are bifurcated into "regular decisions" and "memorandum decisions." Regular decisions involve a novel application of law. Memorandum decisions simply involve the application or interpretation of existing law. Regular decisions often form the basis of precedent that is referred to in future cases.

Taxpayers desiring jury trials can initiate action in the U.S. District Courts. At least one federal district court exists per state, and jurisdiction is often determined by where the taxpayer lives or works. The downside to seeking a hearing in U.S. District Court is that any disputed tax monies must first be paid to the IRS, and then a refund must be sued for in court. District Court cases are handled by a single judge, and a jury trial can be requested.

The U.S. Court of Federal Claims has broad jurisdiction over matters of claims against the U.S. government. Once again, any disputed taxes must first be paid, and then a taxpayer can sue the IRS for a refund. Federal Claims cases are heard by a panel of 16 judges. There are no juries in the U.S. Court of Federal Claims.

Decisions made in U.S. Tax Court and U.S. District Courts can be appealed to the regional U.S. Courts of Appeals. Appeals from the U.S. Court of Federal Claims are heard by the U.S. Court of Appeals for the Federal Circuit. The final level in the federal court process is the U.S. Supreme Court. Nine justices are empaneled to hear cases that it agrees to take. The Supreme Court very rarely accepts tax cases.

In most tax matters, the burden of proof rests with the taxpayer. Certain situations can arise whereby the burden shifts to the IRS. The IRS carries the burden of proof in any case on income, gift, estate, or generation skipping tax, as long as the taxpayer has provided credible evidence, has maintained appropriate books and records, and has reasonably complied with IRS requests.

There are multiple standards of proof that taxpayers are held to. These include:

- reasonable basis;
- substantial authority; and
- more likely than not.

Reasonable basis means that a tax position has at least a 20 percent chance of prevailing. This standard can be used to shield a taxpayer from various penalties for underpayment of tax, including the negligence penalty and the penalty for disregarding rules or regulations, as long as the taxpayer acted in good faith and did not have willful neglect. Reasonable basis can be argued to avoid the substantial underpayment penalty only if the tax position is disclosed.

Penalties can only be avoided for an undisclosed tax position if the position meets the substantial authority standard. The substantial authority standard is met with a tax position that has more than a 40 percent chance of succeeding in court. The following can be used to assert substantial authority:

1. applicable provisions of the IRC and other statutory provisions;
2. proposed, temporary, and final regulations construing such statutes;
3. revenue filings and revenue procedures, tax treaties, and regulations;
4. court cases;
5. congressional intent as reflected in committee reports, joint explanatory statements of managers included in conference committee reports, and floor statements made prior to enactment by one of a bill's managers;
6. general explanations of tax legislation prepared by the joint (U.S. Senate and U.S. House of Representatives) Committee on Taxation (the "Blue Book");
7. private letter rulings and technical advice memoranda issued after October 31, 1978;
8. actions on decisions and general counsel memoranda issued after March 12, 1981 (as well as general counsel memoranda published in pre-1955 volumes of the Cumulative Bulletin); and
9. IRS information or press releases and notices, announcements, and other administrative pronouncements published by the IRS in the Internal Revenue Bulletin.

In order to meet the more likely than not standard, a tax position must have a greater than 50 percent chance of being confirmed in a theoretical court trial. The benefits of an uncertain tax position that meets the more likely than not standard are that it can be recognized on the taxpayer's financial statements. Otherwise, failing to meet this standard most properly prevents recognition of the benefit in financials that are filed with the IRS.

The operative standard, for the purposes of this analysis, is the more likely than not standard. Nonetheless, forms of authoritative guidance that qualify for the substantial authority standard can be used as part of the compliance process with the more likely than not standard. The additional 10 percent certainty difference between them relates to the applicability of the guidance to a specific position.

Our previous analysis of UBTI in Chapter 5 discussed Revenue Ruling 80-296, in which the IRS decided in favor of an athletic conference by finding that it was not subject to UBTI for the sale of broadcasting rights to an annual competition. Specifically, the IRS ruled that "...the sale of the broadcasting rights and the resultant broadcasting of the game contributes importantly to the accomplishment of the organization's exempt purpose."[1] The exempt purpose being described is education, for which the constituent colleges and universities of the athletic conference qualified as charities.

As a revenue ruling, this decision represents substantial authority, and thus the college athletics industry would have at least a 40 percent chance of prevailing in a tax dispute by referencing this position. Does it rise to the standard of more likely than not? It was issued in 1980, so being more than 40 years old may weaken its credibility. To have certainty of meeting the more stringent more likely than not standard, additional evidence might be required.

In a technical guide on UBTI published on December 15, 2023 by the IRS—which formed the basis for the analysis on UBTI in Chapter 5—the IRS discussed Revenue Ruling 80-296. The text used to describe the precedent set by the revenue ruling was regrettably uninspiring:[2]

> "The Service has traditionally taken the position that income from admissions to college and university athletic events isn't income from unrelated business because the events themselves are related to the educational purposes of the colleges and universities."

Through this statement, the technical guide clearly recognizes admissions income as exempt from UBTI, but it seems to walk back guidance provided in Revenue Ruling 80-296 stating that the sale of broadcasting rights would also avoid treatment as UBTI. Technical guides, like revenue rulings, constitute substantial authority. The intent of the text in this guide is unclear, but it may weaken the applicability of Revenue Ruling 80-296 to future situations.

The most recent guidance on the topic was provided by a general counsel memorandum dated May 23, 2023, concerning the operation of NIL collectives. While it cannot be cited as precedent, as a general counsel memorandum, it does represent substantial authority. Its determination on NIL collectives was made abundantly clear in its conclusion statement:[3]

> "An organization that develops paid NIL opportunities for student athletes will, in many cases, be operating for a substantial nonexempt purpose—serving the private interests of student-athletes—which is more than incidental to any exempt purpose furthered by the activity."

While the general counsel memorandum denies exemption to NIL collectives, the text of the memorandum provides a window into the logic used by the IRS to determine charitable purpose, especially as it concerns college athletics.

Regarding exemption under the IRC, the memorandum goes on to state:[3]

> "Treas. Reg SS 1.501(c)(3)-1(c)(1) provides that an organization will be regarded as operated exclusively for one or more exempt purposes only if it engages primarily in activities which accomplish one or more of such exempt purposes specified in section 501(c)(3). An organization will not be so regarded if more than an insubstantial part of its activities is not in furtherance of an exempt purpose."

Here, the memorandum makes a distinction between organizations whose activities are wholly charitable and those where a "more than insubstantial" amount of existence does not further an exempt purpose. "More than insubstantial" is not quantified, but the memo goes on to explain:[3]

> "Treas. Reg. SS 1.501(c)(3)-1(d)(1)(ii) provides that an organization is not organized and operated exclusively for exempt purposes unless it serves a public rather than a private interest. To meet this requirement, an organization must establish that it is not organized or operated for the benefit of private interests such as designated individuals, the creator or his family, shareholders of the organization, or persons controlled, directly or indirectly, by such private interests."

NIL collectives—as their activities predominantly benefit individual athletes rather than a broader charitable purpose—do not qualify for exemption. The memo further asserts that determining whether an entity is organized and operated exclusively for an exempt purpose is effected through an operational test using the "private benefit doctrine," as stated as follows:[3]

> "The operational test is designed to ensure that an organization's resources and activities are devoted to furthering those exempt purposes...Whether an

organization is operated exclusively for exempt purposes depends on the facts and circumstances. However, an organization bears the burden of proof to establish that it is not operated for the benefit of private interests."

Once again, the taxpayer most often bears the burden of proof in a position. In cases like this, it is the taxpayer who must properly ascertain compliance with the operational test as it concerns the private benefit doctrine by citing substantial authority combined with the particular facts and circumstances of an individual situation:[3]

"Under the operational test, the purpose toward which an organization's activities are directed, and not the nature of the activities themselves, is ultimately dispositive of whether an organization is described in Section 501(c)(3). An activity may be engaged in for more than one purpose (a dual-purpose activity). However, a single nonexempt purpose, if substantial in nature, will preclude exemption regardless of the number or importance of truly exempt purposes."

The previous excerpt is key, because it underscores the fact that nonexempt activities that are substantial to the organization's operations are sufficient to void the exemption even in the presence of multiple additional properly charitable activities.

The definition of "substantial" in accounting is fluid, as the term is used in many contexts. One scenario in which it is utilized is for the determination of a going concern. In this situation, auditors must offer a notation in their audit opinion for a set of financial statements if there is "substantial doubt" about a company's ability to meet its financial obligations in a timely manner one year from the date the audit report is issued. Substantial doubt in this situation is typically regarded as a greater than 50 percent chance. It is then easily surmised that anything comprising 50 percent or more of an organization's activities would be considered substantial.

In the matter of discussion, however, 50 percent seems too liberal. Obviously, anything comprising most of a group's operations is substantial. If we conflate "substantial" with "significant," we arrive at the significant influence standard used in the principles of consolidation in financial accounting. Here, a company that exercises "significant influence" over another corporate organization is required to use something called equity method consolidation to present the influenced company's results on its income statement and balance sheet. Significant influence in this case is commonly defined as a 20 percent or greater ownership stake. A good rule of thumb for "substantial," therefore, in the subtext of nonexempt activities would be anything that comprises 20 percent or more of an entity's operations.

Further discussion on the operational test, providing for both its qualitative and quantitative components, continues as follows:[3]

...when evaluating an organization's qualification for exemption, it is necessary to determine whether the organization's activity furthers an exempt purpose or a nonexempt purpose, or both, and if the activity furthers both an exempt and nonexempt purpose, whether the nonexempt purpose is incidental to the exempt purpose such that the organization nevertheless qualifies for exemption under 501(c)(3)."

Therefore, for nonexempt activities to be acceptable to an entity that nonetheless qualifies as a charity under Section 501(c)(3), they must be "incidental" in nature. The concept of incidental is further explained in the memo:[3]

"To be qualitatively incidental, the private benefit must be a byproduct of the exempt activity or a necessary concomitant to the accomplishment of the exempt purpose. Private benefit that is not qualitatively incidental might also be described as direct or intentional."

Private benefit as a "byproduct" or "necessary concomitant" is either an unavoidable consequence or a necessary catalyst to the exempt purpose. This forms the qualitative basis of the operational test.

Adding detail to the quantitative aspect of the operational test, the memo continues with an example:[3]

"To be quantitatively incidental, the private benefit must be insubstantial in amount when compared to the overall public benefit conferred by the activity. For example, in Rev. Rul.76-152, a group of art patrons formed an organization to promote community understanding of modern art trends by exhibiting and selling the work of local artists at an art gallery. The organization retained a 10% commission on sales and turned over 90 percent of the sales proceeds to the individual artists. The revenue ruling concluded that the benefit to the artists could not be considered quantitatively incidental to the organization's exempt purposes."

In the aforementioned example, 90 percent is certainly substantial by any definition. Previously, this analysis asserted that 20 percent was a good benchmark for substantiality, so the art gallery was in excess of that threshold by 4.5 times.

To conclude on the operational test, the IRS summarizes:[3]

"As stated above, private benefit resulting from an organization's activities must be both qualitatively and quantitatively incidental to find that an organization is not serving private interests more than incidentally. In other words, an activity that benefits private interests in a manner that is qualitatively incidental does not further exempt purposes if the benefit to private interests is quantitatively substantial. Similarly, if an activity provides a direct or intentional benefit to private interests such that it is not qualitatively incidental, it does not matter that the benefit may be quantitatively insubstantial: the direct private benefit is deemed repugnant to the idea of an exclusively public charitable purpose."

In essence, nonexempt activities must be both incidental and insubstantial in order to be conducive to an organization achieving and maintaining charitable status under Section 501(c)(3) of the IRC. Moreover, in its summation on the operational test, the IRS highlights the fact that even insubstantial nonexempt activities can preclude exemption if they intentionally benefit a private interest.

It can be argued that the current manifestation of intercollegiate athletics, even post-settlement, would pass the operational test on both a qualitative and quantitative basis. To the extent that this holds, it likely means the current tax position of the NCAA, conferences, and the host institutions would meet the more likely than not standard and fulfill its burden of proof to the IRS. As such, its financials can continue to reflect exemption from federal income taxes.

Qualitatively, any private benefit derived from NIL activities is certainly incidental to the broader exempt purpose of college athletics. NIL would not qualify as being a necessary concomitant to the existence of college athletics, but it is a byproduct of an industry that provides exponential public benefit. Rather than being intentional or direct, the NIL phenomenon has emerged as an unavoidable consequence of a pursuit that has become highly commercialized as a result of its success. As such, there is a very strong argument that NIL benefits are qualitatively incidental to the exempt purpose(s) of college sports.

From a quantitative perspective, NIL revenues are currently derived outside the scope of the official organizations of intercollegiate athletics. Boosters provide the capital that gets distributed to athletes in exchange for the use of their NIL. In this way, the NIL benefits are external to the college sports industry proper, making them by default insubstantial.

Post-settlement, in order to fulfill revenue-sharing promises, certain proceeds from conference distributions will likely be directed to NIL activities, thereby internalizing a portion of the private benefit created by NIL. Under the terms of the settlement, this revenue sharing will, perhaps coincidentally or uncoincidentally, be limited to 22 percent of a particular institution's conference distributions. Therefore, it should be close enough to the 20 percent standard to remain below the threshold established in this analysis for substantiveness.

Moreover, the various additional revenue streams that drive college sports will further dilute the percentage represented by internalized NIL. According to the Knight Commission, NCAA and conference distributions, media rights and post-season football represent 28 percent of total revenues for the entire FBS.[4] Even if the maximum 22 percent of this was diverted to revenue sharing, this would only represent 6.2 percent of the total revenue for the FBS; this is well within the threshold for it to be considered insubstantial.

In conclusion, therefore, using the operational test outlined in a very recent general counsel memorandum provided by the IRS, the expected impact of private benefits in college sports will remain incidental and insubstantial, thereby preserving exemption.

Furthermore, given that this memorandum represents substantial authority—and a thorough analysis has confirmed that it applies to the situation at hand—the intercollegiate athletics industry meets its burden of proof for the exempt position under the more likely than not standard. As long as the validity of this position persists, the college sports industry will be free to pursue its exempt purposes without tax burden.

As discussed in this literary piece, the exempt purposes of college athletics are twofold: (1) nonprofessional (amateur) sports and (2) education. The latter has been specifically cited by the IRS on more than one occasion as constituting the basis for its upholding the exempt status of the various industry principals, including the NCAA, conferences, and member institutions. Returning to the general counsel memo, it states:[3]

> "Student-athletes themselves are not a recognized charitable class. While the Service has previously recognized as charitable certain organizations whose activities benefited student-athletes, the rulings were based on a determination that the activities advanced education."

This statement by the general counsel memorandum is congruent with Revenue Ruling 80-296 from more than 40 years ago. This ruling determined that the sale of broadcasting rights for an intercollegiate tournament "contributes importantly" to the exempt purpose of the conferences' membership, which consisted of colleges and universities recognized as charities for their pursuit of education.

It is agreed that college sports contribute importantly to education—but what about their advancement of amateur sports? Especially for those nonrevenue sports that are featured prominently in the Olympics, this is an important contribution made by the industry to the greater good of the country. This is why the TRA of 1976 was passed. Has the IRS simply forgotten about this?

Not likely. Rather, it can be argued that the conformity of the college athletics industry to the definition of amateurism under federal law, which we have termed nonprofessionalism, is the predicate condition for its contributing importantly to education; that is, education is the second order effect of nonprofessionalism. While college sports technically have two exempt purposes, one could not exist without the other.

The IRS has aptly avoided discussing this equation, likely due to the nature of the accounting profession in the United States. U.S. GAAP is a rule-based system focused on relatively strict interpretation of reporting guidelines and protocol. Abroad, the use of IFRS, which is a principle-based system, is more common. Principle based systems focus more on ultimate congruence to the concepts of fair presentation and disclosure than adherence to tightly written rules. Tax accounting is an even purer rule-based system than GAAP. As examined herein, amateurism is a loosely defined principle, whose definition—even under federal law—is fluid based on the caprice of international athletics committees. Hence, there is the analysis of nonprofessionalism. Rather than get into that, it is far easier for the IRS to simply create a rule about whether something is educational or not. The Merriam-Webster Dictionary defines *education* as follows:[4]

> "The field of study that deals mainly with methods of teaching and learning in schools."

With this as a rule, given the fact that student athletes are full-time students in school—and their activities predominantly benefit their institutions and other member institutions—their pursuits are certainly educational in nature.

Conversely, if these student athletes were professionalized, their endeavors would no longer comply with this rule. It is very difficult to argue that professional sports are educational. Their purpose, as professional for-profit private sector industries, is to provide profit to their owners and, by extension, to the coaches and players as well. Any educational benefit they provide is peripheral to their primary objective of enriching their principals. Moreover, it would be extremely difficult for athletes to remain full-time students and simultaneously play professionally for their institutions. In this way, they would no longer be "in school" and would be outside of the scope of education.

Therefore, if the college athletics industry was professionalized through the establishment of employer–employee relationships between the member institutions and the players, it would no longer be able to pass the operational test for exemption under IRC Section 501(c)(3). Qualitatively, the industry would go from providing public benefit to intentionally creating private benefits for a nonexempt class of individuals. The quantitative impact of such an occurrence is discussed in the next chapter, and suffice it to say, it is not insubstantial.

Key takeaways from this chapter include:

1. The college sports industry, like any taxpayer, bears the burden of proof for its tax position and must meet the more likely than not standard to continue to claim exemption in its financials.

2. Recent guidance from the IRS provides for an operational test whereby any private benefit derived from a charitable activity must be qualitatively incidental and quantitatively insubstantial in order for an organization to remain exempt under Section 501(c)(3).

3. Under its current and post-settlement manifestation, the intercollegiate athletics industry can continue to meet the burden of proof under the more likely than not standard that its activities predominantly serve one or more exempt purposes. This would no longer be the case in a professionalized model.

Effects of Taxation

The event whereby the industry of college sports loses its tax exemption will be far from inconsequential for all participants. Both large and small programs will be affected. Moreover, both revenue and nonrevenue sports, will be impacted. Players, coaches, fans, and educators will all wake up in a new world that will look and feel much different than the current manifestation of the industry. With few exceptions, these changes will be wholly negative.

Herein, two scenarios for the professionalization of college athletics are analyzed. In the first scenario, the professionalization of the revenue sports is assumed, with nonrevenue sports remaining nonprofessional. The second scenario provides an analysis of the professionalization of all intercollegiate athletics, including revenue and nonrevenue teams. Both scenarios would be detrimental to the NCAA, conferences, and member institutions.

The first scenario envisions that the college athletics industry be able to limit the contagion of professionalization to revenue sports. In this situation, the member institutions would hire football and basketball players as employees while leaving the remainder of their athletes as grant-in-aid students. As will be shown, the expense of these professionalized programs would increase dramatically, and certain sources of revenue would be eliminated. Their ability to subsidize nonrevenue sports would be drastically reduced, if not eradicated.

Assuming college football and basketball were professionalized, they would most certainly be subject to UBTI. This would translate into their income being taxed at the corporate federal tax rate, which is currently 21 percent. Under changes made to Section 512 (a) by the Tax Cuts and Jobs Act of 2017, which added Section 512 (a) (6), entities running multiple unrelated businesses must calculate UBTI separately for each unrelated activity. As such, the taxable income for an institution's football and basketball programs would need to be calculated separately, with the tax applicable to their income, before any distributions could be made to nonrevenue programs. This would reduce their ability to subsidize the broader athletics department by at least 21 percent. In many states, generating UBTI also subjects the unrelated business to state income taxes. In the United States, corporate income tax is imposed in 44 states with top marginal rates ranging from 2.5 percent to 9.8 percent.[1] It is thus a material added burden for schools operating in certain states.

Taxation would affect an industry already reeling from the promises made in the recently announced NCAA settlement. In that settlement, the NCAA indicated that it would allow revenue sharing of up to 22 percent of conference proceeds, which are predominantly generated by the revenue sports that drive lucrative broadcasting agreements. In transition to a post-settlement, post-professionalized world for college athletics, up to 22 percent of revenue could be diverted to revenue-sharing arrangements, while at least 21 percent (or more if state taxes were included) of income after expenses would be due for UBTI taxes.

Expenses would also rise significantly in a professional environment for college athletics. Scholarships would be replaced or supplemented with salaries and bonuses paid to players. Subsequently, the overall cost of maintaining these programs would increase materially.

Average tuition at a public university for the 2023–2024 academic year was $10,662 for in-state students and $23,630 for out-of-state students.[2] For a football team with a 50-person roster, this equates to a total expense of roughly $1.2 million, assuming all of the players are out-of-state students, which is rarely the case. Adding Alston payments of $5,980, this increases to $1.5 million. If one includes a basketball team with 15 players, total scholarship and Alston expenses for revenue sports would be $1.9 million annually.

In a professionalized environment, employee players would likely be paid commensurate to what they could earn elsewhere based on free market dynamics. This would be unlikely to equate to what professionals in premium leagues, like the NFL or NBA, earn. A better proxy would be sub-leagues such as the NBA G League, Arena Football League, and Xtreme Football League (XFL). Standard G League contracts are for $35,000 ($7,000 per month for a 5-month season).[3] Certain select players are paid more, with some eligible for bonuses of up to $50,000.[3] XFL base salaries are $59,000.[4]

Given the fact that on an after-tax basis, these salaries would barely cover tuition, there would need to be a scholarship component that remained in order for the arrangement to make sense from a cash perspective. Adding the cost of covering tuition to an assumed $60,000 annual salary for each player—and a 65-person payroll for football and basketball—drives total player expenses to $5.8 million, nearly triple their current cost.

Even at these elevated levels, it may be difficult to contain spiraling personnel costs. This is especially true if players unionize and engage in collective bargaining activity to push for higher wages. It would likely be the case—as discussed in a prior chapter—that based on updated NLRB guidance, employee players could argue entitlement to overtime and other benefits. Further, the natural competitive dynamic of the college athletics environment could drive up salaries as programs seek to attract top talent.

While $5.8 million may not seem like a large number in the grand scheme of college athletics, in aggregate the tripling of personnel expenses would not be a trivial matter. Even at a major Big Ten program like the University of Wisconsin, which spent $40 million on its football program in 2023, this would represent a cost increase of roughly 10 percent.[5]

On a higher level, the FBS collectively spent $2.8 billion on football expenditures in 2023.[5] Assuming 12 percent of this is spent on athletic student aid, which is in line with the broader revenue for FBS institutions severally, this would equate to roughly $331 million.[5] If this number were to triple, it would mean the personnel costs for FBS football alone would be about $1 billion. Higher player costs of this staggering sum would severely impact programs big and small across the FBS. Moreover, it is likely that certain institutions with less developed programs would find it extremely difficult to field football teams given prohibitive costs.

Professionalized college football and basketball would therefore be beset by numerous cost increases. First, the industry has already promised to divert up to 22 percent of media and broadcasting rights to revenue-sharing arrangements. In addition, having players on payroll in football and basketball programs could drive a threefold increase in player costs. Moreover, any revenue left over after a 22 percent haircut on media rights intake, and a rise by 3 times in player costs, would be further subject to UBTI taxation before it could be distributed to nonrevenue sports. Minimally, based on current federal tax rates, this would involve a 21 percent reduction in the bottom line, with potential for additional liability for state taxes. At the very least, this would cripple the ability of revenue sports to subsidize nonrevenue sports, such that the latter at many institutions may need to become self-funding.

Even this outcome assumes that the NCAA, conferences, and member institutions are able to stem the contagion of professionalization to revenue sports. This is a big assumption, especially given Title IX requirements to provide equitable treatment to men's and women's sports. To the extent that professionalization is viewed as being more favorable vis-à-vis sports that remain nonprofessional, this could be viewed as a Title IX violation, especially as revenue sports are predominantly made up of men's teams. If nonrevenue sports successfully lobbied under Title IX to be treated in the same manner as revenue sports, the entire industry would be professionalized.

The cost of such a phenomenon would likely be unbearable. Division I FBS and FCS combine to include over 30,000 student athletes nationally. Those two conferences currently spend $1.6 billion on athletic student aid.[5] If this cost were to triple in the same manner as in the football and basketball only example, the total cost to those conferences for player personnel would reach $4.7 billion. For the FCS, the new price tag of more than $1.0 billion would represent more than two-thirds of its total subdivision revenue. For the FBS, player costs would rise from roughly 12 percent to 36 percent of revenue. It is clear under this scenario that substantial cuts to programming would need to be enacted.

And this is only the beginning. Along with higher expenses, professionalized college sports would also be estranged from revenue sources available exclusively to charitable organizations. Based on Knight Commission data, the sources of revenue for member institutions in the FBS include:[5]

1. NCAA/conference distributions, media rights, and postseason football: 28 percent;
2. donor contributions: 22 percent;
3. ticket sales: 15 percent;
4. institutional/government support: 12 percent;
5. corporate sponsorship, advertising, and licensing: 9 percent;
6. other revenue: 7 percent;
7. student fees: 5 percent; and
8. competition guarantees: 1 percent.

Apparent from the data is the fact that donor contributions make up the second largest source of revenue for FBS programs. Following the loss of charitable status, college sports would no longer be able to solicit tax-deductible contributions. With donors unable to avail themselves of the tax savings from contributing, donations would likely dry up rapidly. In 2023, this revenue stream represented more than $2.3 billion that would likely be lost in a professionalized model.

In addition to donations, it is unlikely that governments would allocate taxpayer dollars to a for-profit enterprise. Further, institutions could likely not support professionalized programs without incurring significant UBTI expenses. In 2023, institutional and government support represented 12 percent of total FBS revenues. Student fees, at 5 percent of revenues, likely could no longer be appropriated to what would become essentially a private sector endeavor.

For FBS institutions collectively, these foregone sources of revenue represented $4.2 billion in 2023, or 39 percent of a $10.6 billion top line.[5] These line items comprised 77 percent of FCS school revenues in the same time period, with most coming from institutional and government support, followed by student fees as the next most significant source.[5] FCS member institutions would lose $1.1 billion and be estranged from over three-quarters of their revenue.[5] Educational establishments in the No Football Subdivision derived 58 percent of their revenue from these sources in 2023 and would stand to lose $472 million that they can ill afford to give up.[5] This brings the total bill for forfeited revenue under a professionalized model to $5.7 billion across the FBS, FCS, and No Football Subdivision. With this type of hit, expenses would certainly need to be cut.

Smaller schools would bear the highest cost of such a phenomenon with both the FCS and No Football Subdivision being dispossessed of a supermajority and majority of their revenue sources, respectively. Severe cuts to programs would likely need to result, with nonrevenue sports likely the first targets. It can be expected that certain schools with thinner resources may need to exit intercollegiate athletics altogether. With many lesser-known regional institutions already facing declining enrollment, it can be foreseen that the loss of college sports could be the last blow that pushes them into dissolution.

Hemorrhaging this amount of cash would certainly not leave the larger programs unscathed either. As shown as follows, nearly all of the proceeds received by big-time college athletics are earmarked for various expenses. For the FBS, these include:[5]

facilities and equipment: 22 percent;
coaches' compensation: 19 percent;
support and admin compensation: 18 percent;
game expenses and travel: 12 percent; and
recruiting: 2 percent.

While certain expenses (like coaches' salaries and travel costs) are unavoidable, facilities and equipment would be an easy target for cutbacks, especially as they represented a material 22 percent of fund outflows for the FBS.[5] Gone would be the dazzling facilities that college sports fans have gotten used to enjoying, as they would likely be replaced with cheaper venues. In established schools, as well as smaller institutions, there would almost certainly be need for a reduction in program offerings, with nonrevenue sports bearing the brunt of reductions.

In this austere environment, the experience of intercollegiate athletics would be vastly altered. With fans deriving less enjoyment from following their favorite teams, the industry would likely see further revenue contraction as broadcasting and mass media rights declined in value. The industry of college athletics has already been experiencing some saturation, and the NCAA and conferences have shelved plans to add more regular season games, as they see the market as fully penetrated. The advent of professionalism would therefore have a deleterious effect on a pastime that has already peaked in popularity.

A professionalized model is also something that the industry of intercollegiate athletics is unlikely to grow into. The Division I FBS, FCS, and No Football

Subdivision generated a total of $12.9 billion of revenue in 2023.[5] Here is how they break down:

FBS: $10.6 billion;
FCS: $1.4 billion;
No Football Subdivision: $815 million; and
total: $12.9 billion.

Comparatively, the NFL alone generated $20.2 billion in revenue in 2023, which was more than all of college sports combined. Together, the NFL, the NBA, Major League Baseball (MLB), and the National Hockey League (NHL) produced a whopping $48.9 billion in top line receipts in 2023. Here is how they break down:[6]

NFL: $20 billion;[6]
MLB: $11 billion;
NBA: $11.3 billion (2023/24 season); and[6]
NHL: $6.4 billion. (2022/23 season)

As is apparent, the professional sports industry, even narrowly defined in this manner, is nearly four times the size of the summation of all intercollegiate athletics. Notable as well is that this calculation of the size of professional sports excludes significant categories, including auto racing, equine contests, and numerous other professional athletic endeavors. Suffice it to say, the business of professional sports is a behemoth enterprise, whereas the industry of college athletics is somewhat of a niche industry.

While the professional athletics industry is many times larger than that of college sports, it is comprised of far fewer organizations and players, translating into lower overhead. The NFL consists of 32 teams, MLB and the NBA have 30 teams each, and the NHL fields 32 teams. These 124 teams employ just under 6,000 professional athletes.[7] Compare this to the FBS, which alone has 130 members, with the FCS adding an additional 125.[8] If the 97 Division 1, No Football (formerly referred to as D1-AAA) schools are added, this jumps to 350.[8] FBS schools are required to sponsor a minimum of 16 sports, while FCS schools must maintain 14. Assuming only the minimum number of required teams and a plug of 10 sports for the "no football" schools, this amounts to a total of nearly 5,000 individual sports teams. Collectively, these programs have more than 190,000 student athletes on their rosters in any given year.[8]

Further, professional sports facilities are often financed by public funds such as municipal general obligation bonds. This makes the athletic franchises themselves relatively capital light. This is not so for college athletics, whose educational institutions must solicit donations and securitize pledges to build the stunning 100,000+ seat football stadiums and immaculate basketball arenas replete with luxury amenities and suites. While the professional sports arena makes up for this more efficient cost structure with massive compensation packages, this is mostly discretionary, whereas the burden for intercollegiate athletics is comprised of significantly more fixed costs.

In professionalization, not only would the U.S. institution of intercollegiate athletics be substantially diminished, but the collateral effect of the reduction in—and, in some cases, the elimination of—nonrevenue sports would be a further deadweight loss to society. Only a small percentage of the population could ever dream of competing in revenue sports and being featured on primetime television. Most athletes compete in nonrevenue sports like swimming, tennis, track and field, and many other lifetime sports. Depriving student athletes of this experience and opportunity will have long-term effects that we can barely conceive of at this point in time. Sports teach critical skills, such as teamwork and competitive ethics, which some believe are unfortunately in decline in today's world. Their reduced availability in higher education will merely exacerbate these supposed trends.

In this way, U.S. institutes of higher learning would lose the significant educational value that intercollegiate athletics provides. The IRS recognizes this value and has heretofore ruled that the industry is deserving of its exemption due to the educational benefit it provides. Purposefully allowing this exemption to be nullified through professionalization is at best a logical non-sequitur and, in more likelihood, an act of lunacy.

Moreover, the decreased prevalence of nonrevenue sports would likely have a material negative impact on the ability of the United States to compete effectively in international athletics. This was the original motivation behind the TRA of 1976 that created the exemption for amateur sports. With fewer colleges offering the nonrevenue sports that are featured in the Olympics, there will be a smaller pool of talent for U.S. Olympic teams to choose from.

In the 2020 Tokyo Olympic games, roughly 75 percent of the more than 600 athletes on Team USA had competed in college athletics.[8] According to the NCAA, its member institutions spend more than $5 billion on Olympic sports annually.[8] As previously analyzed, this is money that would substantially evaporate in a professionalized model. This would be particularly detrimental to U.S. athletic competitiveness internationally, because unlike other countries, the United States. does not contribute directly to the USOPC, but rather it relies on colleges to incubate Olympic athletes.[8]

As such, the professionalization of intercollegiate athletics will have implications beyond the industry of college sports into other U.S. institutions, including our Olympic competitiveness. More than money is therefore on the line; our pride and honor as a country is at stake.

While this discussion and analysis has focused on Division I schools, there will no doubt be an impact on Division II and III institutions as well. Similar to smaller FCS and No Football Subdivision schools, certain establishments under this category are already struggling with declining enrollment and uncertain finances. Sports are a big draw for any institute of higher education. As such, the loss of their appeal—either through being downgraded or outright eliminated—could be the last straw for these schools.

For the larger, well-known programs, it may be possible to offset certain financial consequences with other sources of revenue. In 2023, corporate sponsorships accounted for 9 percent of the revenue earned in the FBS. This channel could be expanded for those schools with sufficient brand recognition to attract large sponsors. Institutions may even be able to solicit investments from private equity firms and other capital vehicles. The issue of how the business model would work, however, would need to be resolved and replacements found for the substantial amount of revenue that would be lost to professionalization—and don't expect this be easy. Fully privatized college sports would nonetheless be a different and likely downgraded experience regardless. There is no guarantee that the model could be tweaked to allow the programs to become profitable enterprises.

In conclusion, the tax implications of professionalizing college athletics, along with the second-order effects of forfeited revenue, would be profound. It is important for this to be understood before influential forces advocate for this to occur. In the end, it would benefit virtually no one and hurt many. Hurt the most would be student athletes from less privileged backgrounds, who would face diminished prospects for participation in intercollegiate athletics. For many, this would severely impact the potential to pursue a career in professional athletics as players, coaches, or management personnel.

Given this reality, the question emerges as to why there would be any interest in going down this path. Hopefully, the preceding analysis will serve as an eye-opener for those seeking to professionalize college sports and hopefully dissuade them from further advocacy. In the next chapter, a theorized motive among certain proponents of this course of action is analyzed.

Key takeaways from this chapter:

1. Any scenario for the professionalization of college athletics would likely result in the loss of tax exemption and the imposition of UBTI taxation at both the state and federal levels.

2. Revocation of charitable status would further result in the truncation of certain revenue sources, such as donor contributions, relying on tax deductions. The cost of this would be exceptionally high.

3. The program reductions necessitated by the increased tax expense and loss of revenue would fundamentally alter the experience of college sports for the worse. Smaller, lesser-known institutions would be hit the hardest, with some of them potentially folding as a result.

12

The Bigger Issue

As discussed in previous chapters, U.S. college sports emerged from an emulation of similar systems across the pond in Great Britain. This ultimately drove the concept of volunteerism that pervaded the debate around college athletics for decades thereafter. Such origins may also underlie certain motivations to professionalize college athletics. This is a relatively benign mentality that unfortunately makes bad company with a more pernicious philosophy catalyzing the advocacy for radical changes to the industry.

The British Empire is credited with sponsoring the spread of athletic activity across the world in one of its most important contributions to the globe.[1] European football (soccer) was invented in England, with some of the earliest matches in the late 19th century.[1] Cricket and rugby evolved around the same time, with the latter founded at the Rugby School in England in 1823.[1] The former is theorized to have originated in 13th century England before being officially organized 700 years later.[1]

American football, as it is well known, was derived from English rugby. Broadly, as mentioned in Chapter 3, U.S. college sports came about through a desire to replicate the perceived athleticism of British youth. The English private school system encouraged athletic as well as academic fitness in its mission to develop future leaders. Universities protracted this emphasis. This led, in the United States, to somewhat of an inferiority complex, resulting in the establishment of gymnasiums and ultimately rowing and rugby clubs that formed the first intercollegiate athletic organizations.

Receiving monetary compensation for participating in athletics at school or at a university is something that would have been anathema to the British in the late 19th century. Not the least of the reasons for this is because those engaging in these activities were predominantly part of the English nobility. In aspiring to compete with the British in this realm, the United States inherited a sense of volunteerism, whereby athletes would forego any potential monetary benefit for competing on behalf of an educational institution.

Even 100 years after the American Revolution, there was an aversion to inheriting British customs. This was not about the British people themselves, but rather it was about certain institutions characteristic of the Empire, such as the class system, aristocracy, and perceived elitism. College athletics, having been derived from sports played at English educational establishments, may have inadvertently been caught up in this trend of shedding Anglo influences.

Nonetheless, it has been more than 240 years since the end of the American Revolution, and any elements of British culture that have assimilated themselves into the fabric of U.S. life are likely here to stay. The desire to replace a volunteer English system with a more industrious U.S. format has some merit and is an otherwise benign reason to seek change in the intercollegiate sports industry. At this point, however, it is an obsolete argument.

More pernicious has been a seeming nascent undercurrent of sentiment against college athletics in general that is unrelated to its nonprofessional business model. This philosophy views college sports as an inefficient use of resources that could be better appropriated to applications with a wider benefit to college and university students as a group and to society. It seems to discount heavily the idea that the intercollegiate athletics industry provides value to anyone other than students who actively participate in it on an NCAA member team roster.

These arguments, while still on the fringe in the modern era, have been around for more than a century. They have led successfully to the cancelation of certain athletic programs or the full removal of sports on some campuses. The legacy of these actions remains at these institutions to this day.

In 1907, Swarthmore College was offered a substantial donation by philanthropist Anna T. Jeanes that was contingent upon the college dismantling all intercollegiate athletics.[2] After much serious consideration, the school decided to forego the donation. However, in the year 2000, Swarthmore voted to jettison its football team.

In 2013, Spellman College, a historically black women's liberal arts college in Atlanta, decided to eliminate intercollegiate athletics and withdraw from the NCAA.[3] The college cited the high cost of the programs, which were running at roughly $1 million, and the fact that only 4 percent of the student population participated in its Division III sports programs.[3] Diverting the funds earmarked for sports toward a schoolwide physical education program was seen as a more broad-serving initiative.

Many more institutes of higher learning have parted ways with their football teams. Wikipedia lists more than 150 defunct NCAA college football programs, including more than 60 formerly from Division I schools.[4] A list of these is provided as follows:[4]

American University	Gonzaga University
University of Arkansas at Little Rock	High Point University

Boston University	Hofstra University
Bradley University	U of Illinois, Chicago
California Baptist	Iona University
California State, Fullerton	Jacksonville University
California State, Long Beach	LIU
California State, Northridge	Loyola Marymount University
UC, Riverside	Loyola University Chicago
UC, San Diego	Loyola University Maryland
UC, Santa Barbara	Manhattan College
Canisius University	Marquette University
Creighton University	University of Maryland Eastern Shore
University of Denver	University of Massachusetts, Lowell
DePaul University	Mount Saint Mary's
University of Detroit	University of Nebraska Omaha
Drexel University	Niagara University
U of Evansville	UNC Asheville
Fairfield University	Northeastern University
George Washington	University of the Pacific

Many of these eliminations were done for practical reasons, most of which were financial. For example, American University discontinued football in 1941 because World War II left too few men on campus to fill a roster.[5] However, recent attempts by students to restart the team have met with resistance from the university, in part because of the expense.[5] Similarly, Creighton University mothballed football during the war and cited costs as the reason that it never returned.[6] The University of Arkansas at Little Rock recently nixed plans to restart its football program due to financial constraints.[7] In 1997, Boston University discontinued football due to significant financial losses.[8] The Terriers were unofficially restarted in 2010 as an unaffiliated LLC.[9]

The COVID-19 pandemic accelerated athletic program eliminations due to cost concerns. University of California at Riverside actually considered eliminating all of its athletics in 2021, as finances were strained by COVID-19, and the school earned the inglorious distinction as the country's most subsidized athletics program, with 90 percent of its budget derived from student fees.[10] The school eventually decided against this course of action.

There is concern that this cost cutting could become contagious. John Fry, who previously led Drexel University—which lists itself among those institutions with a defunct college football team—was recently tapped to become president of Temple University. This led to concern that Fry would seek to eliminate college football at Temple as well.[11] The genesis of this concern stems from a 2016 op-ed in *The Wall Street Journal*, in which Fry is quoted as stating that financial losses from college athletics "force universities to divert funding from the fundamental task of educating students."[12] It should be noted that since assuming the role of Temple's president, Fry has released statements affirming his and the University's support and commitment to football. Nonetheless, it is not unimaginable that shifting college presidencies could provide for the migration of academicians who truly see football as a distraction to schools that would not otherwise contemplate interfering with their athletics programs.

Iona College in New Rochelle ended its run in Division I FCS in 2007, after the dissolution of the MAAC football conference, of which it was a founding member.[13] Six MAAC member programs—including Canisius, Fairfield, La Salle, St. Peter's, Siena, and St. John's—had discontinued their football programs, mostly due to cost issues, resulting in the demise of the entire conference.[13] Iona noted that it could not find "equitable opponents" in any other Division I FCS conferences.[13] This illustrates the concern that an increasing number of schools canceling football due to financial pressure could create a cascading failure of conferences. This could force many other schools to discontinue their programs if they cannot find an alternative conference in which to compete. The problem is particularly acute in the conferences outside the Power 5, where schools are more thinly capitalized. These member institutions would be hit the hardest in a professionalized environment.

Beyond costs, there are some ideological underpinnings to certain decisions to eliminate college football. This is especially true as many colleges and universities have, rather than experiencing financial difficulties, been conversely inundated with alumni donations from successful capital campaigns. These endowments—invested heavily in alternative assets classes such as private equity and venture capital—have further generated healthy returns. The result is that a good number of NCAA member institutions are well capitalized to the extent that cost should no longer be an issue when deciding on the persistence of athletic programming. Nonetheless, cost is clearly not the only issue in these decisions.

In 1940, the University of Chicago canceled its Maroons football team. The decision was made bye President Robert Maynard Hutchens, described retrospectively by the University's college magazine as "decidedly unathletic" and quoted as saying, "whenever I get the urge to exercise, I lie down until the feeling passes."[14] Rather than for financial reasons, the program was discontinued due to unfavorable trends in college football broadly and a desire to maintain high academic standards. When the team returned as a club sport in 1960, students staged a sit-in during a game in protest.[14] Football at the University of Chicago did ultimately return to the NCAA as a Division III team.[14]

The year 2012 saw a sports position page in *The Wall Street Journal* that argued for the elimination of college football in the United States. Penned by Buzz Bissinger, the author of *Friday Night Lights*, the piece centers on not only the high cost of intercollegiate football programs and the fact that many are subsidized by their respective institutions' general budgets, but also the fact that a small fraction of students participate in them.[12] Further, the article asserts that college football is a distraction from academics, and its primary beneficiaries are nostalgic alumni and highly compensated coaches.[12] It goes on to highlight the physical dangers of the sport and the taint of recent scandals, such as the Penn State fiasco.[12]

It is important to note that this op-ed predated recent developments such as Alston payments and the ability of players to receive NIL. Student fees and other institutional support systems are only a small source of funds in college athletics broadly, especially in the large FBS schools that tend to be targets for these types of attacks. Nonetheless, there is a deeper issue here. Specifically, Bissinger stated in *The Wall Street Journal* that, "it [college football] has a place in our society, but not on college campuses."[12]

On the heels of this, author and NYU columnist Malcolm Gladwell hosted a forum in which he proposed that large prestigious universities should begin banning college football.[15] His arguments originate from the physical toll that football exacts on players and its link to neurological disorders, such as chronic traumatic encephalopathy, which has garnered significant attention in recent years in college and professional athletics.[15] He has been one of the most outspoken critics of the sport.

Football's occupational hazards are well known. However, the question of whether banning it from colleges would be a move in support of public health is another matter. Hearing from health professionals today, it seems that more people may be suffering from the ill health effects of a lack of activity than from the ill health effects of an activity that carries some risk of injury. Regardless, this is an area in which progress is being made, and parents should retain discretion as to what activities their children will be involved in (versus attempts by certain states to ban football in high school as well).

The theory that football should be banned from colleges due to its cost, however, is a point that lacks validity—and not just because many of the schools have large endowments. At many campuses, especially the ones with large FBS programs, revenue sports such as football subsidize nonrevenue sports that are primarily cost centers. If football were banned, schools would forego the revenue it produces. This, in turn, would lead to an increasing amount of institutional aid, including student fees, being diverted to athletics. Given the current sensitivity around the rising cost of education, this could lead to all college sports being targeted for elimination in the name of expense reduction—not just football.

Unfortunately, with new generations entering higher education, this scenario is not an unthinkable reality. A recent article in *USA Today* suggested that the appeal of sports in general is in decline among members of Generation Z.[16] The article cited a 2021 study discovering that only 23 percent of those in Generation Z described themselves as passionate sports fans, versus 42 percent of millennials, 33 percent of those in Generation X, and 31 percent of baby boomers.[16] Moreover, the same study found that 27 percent of those in Generation Z described themselves as "anti-sports," whereas only single digit percentages of those in prior generations identified as such.[16] Emory professor Michael Lewis commented on the topic by stating, "Part of the lack of Generation Z fandom is due to younger individuals having less intense feelings of group belonging in general."[16]

This 27 percent of Generation Z members are not original in their disdain for sports. In authoritarian states such as Afghanistan, before September 11, sports such as soccer and cricket were banned.[17] These forms of entertainment were seen as valueless and in conflict with the theocracy.[17] In other countries, sports exist purely in the form of international competition and serve as a vehicle for state propaganda.

Even among western nations, most do not have intercollegiate athletic competition that is comparable to that of the United States. In Europe, the United Kingdom is the only country with college sports through its British Universities and Colleges Sport organization.[18] Similarly, Canada maintains two college sports governing bodies: U Sports and the Canadian Collegiate Athletics Association.[18] Surprisingly, Asia has actually made more progress with a preliminary intercollegiate athletics system developing in China, and with Japan forming the Japan Association for University Athletics and Sport.[18]

As such, the industry of intercollegiate athletics is predominantly a U.S. institution. This may be why it is in disfavor with Generation Z, the members of which have been vocal in their malcontent with the United States for prior bad acts. For most U.S. citizens, however, this is a reason to preserve the industry of college sports in its current nonprofessional format. Said differently, it is our patriotic duty to ensure that the industry of college athletics, as it exists today, is available for future generations—and to disallow a minority from inexorably altering it in a way that jeopardizes its existence.

Whatever the motivation is behind the movement to professionalize college sports, it is clear that doing so would have a deleterious effect across the spectrum of institutions and programs. Large and small schools, revenue and nonrevenue sports, players, students, alumni, and the broader fan base would all be made worse off by this maneuver. It is therefore an enigma that anyone would want this.

The student athletes involved in programs that might survive this cataclysm would be compensated at a higher rate than their current scholarships and Alston payments amount to. However, there is not enough revenue in college sports to pay them at the level of professional athletes in the NFL, NBA, MLB, NHL, or other for-profit leagues. This was discussed in the prior chapter—their pay would likely be commensurate to that earned by minor league baseball players and NBA G League participants. Moreover, as full-time employees, college athletes could end up ceding the rights to the NIL value they create while under the employ of the schools. This contrasts with their current status as independent contractors, whereby they retain all of the licenses to their intellectual property. For many student athletes, this equation would leave them materially worse off from a financial perspective. Therefore, this is not something players should be pushing for.

Those in the pro-union camp should not be enthused by this potential development either. Given the storied history of college sports and the track record of scandals involving point shaving and other forms of self-dealing, a newly formed organized labor system in college sports would likely attract some unsavory influences. Especially with online sports betting taking off in the wake of deregulation at the state level, a *de novo* union system in intercollegiate athletics could easily become rife with corruption related to illegal gambling and various forms of graft. Such a phenomenon would be reminiscent of the racketeer-influenced past of organized labor and would taint the movement broadly.

Most importantly, it is obvious from the revenue picture that professional sports are here to stay. They generate an enormous amount of pecuniary value for a multitude of parties, from owners to players, municipalities, media outfits, apparel manufacturers, and so forth. However, the U.S. market cannot support a duplicated professional athletics system, especially if the surveys indicating declining interest in sports among younger generations are correct. This is apparent in the inability of individual professional sports to support more than one dominant league. In an environment where professional and college athletics would be forced to compete for market share and resources, professional sports would win out, and intercollegiate athletics would be severely diminished.

While it is not clear who benefits from the professionalization of college sports, it is nonetheless an outcome that is being forwarded by a handful of activists who have made some progress in the court system. Rather than this be decided in the courts by appointed federal judges, this is an issue that should be addressed with legislation passed by democratically elected representatives in Congress. As it has been in similar state legislative actions, this should be a bipartisan issue. The next chapter delves into the foundation of sound policy on this matter and how it can be put into effect at a national level.

Key takeaways from this chapter include:

1. The industry of intercollegiate athletics has been in the crosshairs of detractors for over a century, with certain institutions taking action to eliminate programs.
2. Numerous colleges and universities have eliminated football, predominantly due to cost issues. Nonetheless, a certain ideology pervades that seeks to undermine the value that college football and other intercollegiate sports add to society.
3. Advocates for professionalization of college sports are either inadvertently or purposefully advancing a system that would have substantial adverse effects on the industry. While the future of professional sports is assured, that of intercollegiate athletics is not so certain.

Sound Policy

In the midst of the chaos that has surrounded college sports over the last several years, there should be sound policy to address the important changes that have occurred and prevent inadvisable alterations to the business model. This penultimate chapter discusses a path forward that intends to preserve intercollegiate athletics in substantially similar form to what has been enjoyed by fans, players, and institutions for decades. It is clear that such policies will need to be adopted at a national level due to the interstate nature of college athletic competition.

While the NCAA has been a pariah among both fans and detractors of college sports for some time, it clearly has a role in administering a landscape of programs that spans hundreds of institutions. Although some of its legislation in the past seemed impractical, its role as a regulator and interface with the public and with various governments will be invaluable to maintaining the virtues of college sports going forward. Much of what NCAA President Charlie Baker is advocating for seeks to legitimize the NCAA as the governing body of college sports, despite the reality that a substantial portion of the revenue is aggregated and distributed by the various conferences, CFP, and bowl organizations, along with other intermediaries.

There are major reasons that policy intervention is required to enable the NCAA to serve in this role. The first is that it has been beset by antitrust lawsuits related to its discharge of authority over conferences and programs. Such actions involve allegations of past as well as current conduct. Its track record defending this litigation has been poor. Legislation will be required if the NCAA is not to be sued out of existence. Secondly, an overriding regulator is even more important now with the advent of NIL and the potential for corrupting influences to emerge, as they did in the past with point shaving and other cheating scandals. Finally, and perhaps most importantly, the labor issue of whether college athletes are employees of their respective member institutions should be resolved in favor of them remaining independent contractors.

Most of the lawsuits filed against the NCAA have alleged antitrust practices. Many of these have been successful, including the recent actions aggregated as part of the watershed NCAA settlement announced in May of 2024. Clearly, in order to avoid future actions of this type and settlements that threaten its status as a going concern, the NCAA must seek some safe harbor from antitrust scrutiny.

Antitrust lawsuits draw their original legislative underpinnings from the Sherman Antitrust Act of 1890. This law was passed by Congress to prohibit trusts, which were arrangements in which shareholders from different companies contributed their stock to single trust managed by a group of trustees.[1] During the time the Act was initiated, such trusts came to exercise monopolistic control over major industries, including oil, which was a sector whose fortunes were essentially dictated by the nine trustees of the Standard Oil Trust.[1] For this reason, the Sherman Antitrust Act was passed to restore fair markets.

Since 1890, the Clayton Act of 1914 expanded the scope of antitrust efforts to include prohibition of tying contracts, certain corporate mergers, and interlocking directorates.[2] The Hart-Scott Rodino Antitrust Improvements Act of 1976 amended the Clayton Act by mandating that advance notice of pending mergers be filed with the Federal Trade Commission and the Antitrust Division of the DOJ for certain mergers.[2] Subsequently, the process codified by the Hart-Scott Rodino Act is the primary means by which mergers and acquisitions are disallowed in the United States.

Today, trusts are colloquially equated with monopolies, even when a trust structure does not exist. Antitrust action has more recently been taken against companies such as Microsoft, Google, MasterCard, and Visa. Alleged monopolies are often accused of conspiracy in restraint of trade, and groups of companies that do not have a control relationship are also targeted for collusion, most often with the intent to fix prices. Jet Blue and Spirit Airways recently terminated their merger after the DOJ sued to block it under the Hart-Scott Rodino Act.[3]

While corporate breakups and stalled mergers get the lion's share of the press, there are certain monopolies that are allowed to persist in the economy. These entities include utility companies, such as power and water companies, as well as firms providing critical infrastructure such as railroads. With no argument that these companies exercise monopolistic influence, they are nonetheless permitted by the government to operate without competition. Although not free from controversy, these special situations are considered "natural monopolies."

A "natural monopoly" is defined in an economics textbook as, "A market situation in which the average costs of production continually decline with increased output. Therefore, average costs of production will be lowest when a single, large firm produces the entire output demanded."[4] Essentially, it is a situation in which a unitary provider can provide the best product or service at the lowest price. For example, given the footprint of utilities like power and water plants, it would be inefficient for several of them to compete in the same geography. Most obvious would be the overlap of power lines and pipes, but there also would be the lack of differentiation that would drive prices to levels that would make it undesirable to provide power. The same is true with rail systems—having multiple systems serving the same routes does not benefit the consumer and would likely result in inefficiencies due to traffic and congestion, as well as adverse price consequences.

Natural monopolies typically exist under extra scrutiny and regulation from government agencies. Prices are often regulated with increases necessitating approval from the appointed regulator. In North Carolina, the North Carolina Utilities Commission is empowered to regulate the rates of all public utilities in the state.[5] The Surface Transportation Board is the independent federal agency entrusted with regulating various modes of surface transportation, predominantly freight rail.[6] Amtrak, officially the National Railroad Passenger Company, was incorporated by an act of Congress in 1970 after the failure of a number of private unregulated railroads.[7] It is regulated by an arm of the U.S. Department of Transportation known as the Federal Railroad Administration.[7]

There is a strong argument that certain spectator sports are natural monopolies. It does not make any more sense to have multiple stadiums in a given metropolis as it does to have numerous train stations or power stations serving the same geography. In fact, in some situations, independent teams will share a single event space, such as the New York Giants and Jets at MetLife Stadium in New Jersey. With sports, the cost of attendance will be lower if teams benefit from the economies of scale of a single stadium. Moreover, for the purposes of an overriding regulator that enforces the rules, this is most effectively accomplished by a single league or commission versus two or more that have differing opinions and judgments.

In 1922, in the case of *Federal Baseball Club v. National League*, the Supreme Court ruled unanimously that MLB was deserving of an exemption from the Sherman Antitrust Act.[8] The controversial decision was upheld in 1953.[8] The reasoning behind this decision was that baseball was an exhibition and not under the auspices of the Commerce Clause.[8] In 2008, Justice Samuel Alito expressed his agreement with the decision, arguing that baseball was not a significant enough form of interstate commerce to warrant subjugation to federal antitrust laws.[8]

Unlike the 1922 case, *Toolson v. New York Yankees*, which was the 1953 challenge to the Supreme Court's earlier decision, was not as universally agreed to.[8] The single paragraph opinion expressed the belief of the majority that Congress was the more appropriate place to settle this dispute.[8] The ruling was, "We think that if there are evils in this field which now warrant application to it of the antitrust laws, it should be by legislation."[8] Two judges dissented with Justice Harold Burton, stating: "Congress, however, has enacted no express exemption of organized baseball from the Sherman Act and no court has demonstrated the existence of an implied exemption from the Act of any sport that is so highly organized as to amount to an interstate monopoly or which restrains interstate trade or commerce."[8]

Flood v. Kuhn in 1972 was the second challenge to the exemption ruling.[8] Curt Flood was contesting baseball's "reserve clause" that prevented players from becoming free agents. In a 5-3 majority decision, the Court ruled against Flood but disclaimed that baseball operated outside of federal antitrust regulation and rather affirmed the prior opinion that Congress was the appropriate arm of the government to take action. Despite being among the majority in the Toolson decision, Justice William O. Douglas dissented in the *Flood* case, stating, "While I joined the Court's opinion in *Toolsen v. New York Yankee, Inc.*, I have lived to regret it; and I now would now correct what I believe to be its fundamental error."[8]

MLB's antitrust exemption was challenged again in 2017 by a group of minor league players arguing that the major league's contract standards suppressed wages.[8] It failed in the Ninth Circuit Appeals Court. The three-person panel referred to the three prior Supreme Court decisions as precedent for their ruling.[8] However, in 1998, the Curt Flood Act partially repealed MLB's antitrust exemption, stating that federal antitrust legislation applied to major league baseball in matters involving employment.[9]

From this legal precedent, it is apparent that if the NCAA were to achieve an antitrust exemption like that enjoyed by MLB, it would need to be accomplished through legislation in Congress. The courts, including the Supreme Court, rightly loathe to legislate from the bench. To the extent that issues surrounding intercollegiate athletics are adjudicated in the federal judicial system, it can be expected that decisions will be predominantly adverse to the NCAA's position. This has indeed been the precedent.

Even prior to the landmark settlement in April, the NCAA had lost many antitrust cases. The most significant, in 1983, disintermediated the NCAA from the lion's share of football revenue. Without federal legislation explicitly providing an exemption for the NCAA from antitrust laws, its discharge of its role as the regulator for college sports will continue to expose it to legal jeopardy. At some point, given its limited resources, the NCAA will become insolvent from the endless litigation and unfavorable legal judgments.

From prior discussion, it was disclosed that the NCAA derives the supermajority of its revenue from its quasi-patented NCAA men's basketball tournament. In 2023, the NCAA produced $1.3 billion in revenue and ended the year with $565 million in net assets.[10] For the fiscal year, $873 million of this was derived from broadcasting rights for the Division I men's basketball tournament.[10] The rights to other championship events added another $73 million.[10] As a nonprofit with revenue tied heavily to these two sources, the NCAA's top line does not grow very significantly from year to year. The NCAA also distributes roughly $600 million annually to Division I member schools and conferences.[11]

The main point is that the NCAA is not a stalworth of resources that can absorb endless litigation, especially when those seeking recourse through the courts are seeking 9- and 10-figure settlements. Future litigation will likely look beyond the NCAA to the conferences and member institutions and will increase the breadth of impact these actions have on college sports broadly. Federal legislation is the only means of preempting this.

In May of 2024, U.S. Representatives Russell Fry (R-SC) and Barry Moore (R-AL), who sit on the House Judiciary Committee, introduced the Protect the Ball Act, which is intended to provide protection for the various organizing bodies of intercollegiate athletics.[12] This legislation would permit the NCAA to act as the central regulator for college sports in affairs such as recruiting, eligibility standards, and NIL.[12] The NCAA would be insulated under this bill from antitrust litigation in the discharge of these regulatory duties.[12] Congressman Fry summed up the impetus for the effort as such: "NIL rules are ever-changing, heavily litigated and essentially unenforceable—causing confusion and chaos for everyone involved. We must establish a liability shield on the national level to protect schools, student-athletes and conferences as they navigate this new set of circumstances. This legislation is an integral component of saving college sports as we know it."[12]

All in, roughly seven bills on this topic have been introduced in the House and the Senate.[12] Some of these were only discussion drafts, but none have really progressed. It is unfortunate, as this should truly be a bipartisan issue. In states that have passed laws to expand NIL collectives, the efforts have received overwhelming support from both sides of the aisle. I am sure if a poll was taken of college athletics fans, there would be substantial representation from both Republicans and Democrats.

Hopefully, through the analysis done in this book, more lawmakers and voters will understand what is at stake. Especially as we move beyond the headlines that have dominated the last half decade—from COVID-19 to election interference, inflation, and economic growth stagnation—this situation should gain more attention. We really need to put the brakes on the current trends persisting in the industry of college sports. We also must make sure these new developments are accompanied by rules and regulations that are commensurate to its being an enhancement to the experience of fans and athletes and not a detriment. Unfortunately, if disorganization continues to spiral out of control, the damage could be hard to reverse.

Primarily, it is going to be critical for the NCAA to be permitted to regulate NIL. Compensation arrangements negotiated with lesser known third parties are fertile ground for potential corrupting influences. We don't want to see the recurrence of scandals reminiscent of the point shaving incidents that occurred in the middle to late part of the last century. The industry of intercollegiate athletics is at a point in its existence where developments such as those would be far less tolerated by the public and government agencies.

NIL regulation will need to address some serious concerns. Some particular concerns are how much coordination will be allowed with member institutions, whether member institutions can contribute directly to NIL collectives, and whether there will be limits on contributions from individuals and businesses. The IRS has already made it unequivocally clear that NIL contributions will not be tax deductible. This puts them in a realm more similar to political campaigns than the charitable organizations that dominate college athletics. In many ways, the NCAA's role will be like that of the Federal Election Commission (FEC).

The FEC was established in 1974 through amendments to the Federal Election Campaign Act.[13] As an independent federal agency, its role is to enforce federal campaign finance laws covering the public financing of presidential campaigns, restrictions on contributions and expenditures made to influence federal elections, and public disclosure of funds raised and spent to influence federal elections.[13] Its mission is to "protect the integrity of the federal campaign finance process by providing transparency and fairly enforcing and administering federal campaign laws."[13]

Federal campaign finance regulations can be complex, but their purpose is relatively straightforward. They are meant to ensure that campaign finances are free from undue influence from a single individual or group of individuals acting in concert; that campaign contributions are disclosed; and that federal election campaigns are devoid of foreign influence. Contributions to candidate campaigns and committees are subject to limits and to disclosure. The same is true for political action committees (PACs). Super PACs are specialized PACs that are not subject to contribution limits but are not permitted to coordinate with candidate campaigns. Only U.S. citizens and permanent residents are eligible to make campaign donations; foreign nationals are strictly forbidden from participating in federal campaign finance.

The NCAA will likely need to set up a FEC-style framework for regulating NIL donor eligibility, disclosure, and any potential limitations. Whether certain types of individuals are enjoined from participating in NIL finance due to conflicts of interest will need to be decided as well. Especially following the controversial dealings between the PGA and LIV Golf, the involvement of foreign capital in the NIL system will need to be discussed, as well as any regulations envisioned. To accomplish this, the NCAA will need to be the beneficiary of strong federal legislation permitting it to function as a governing body for NIL without exposure to antitrust suits.

In addition to NIL, the NCAA will need to be empowered to regulate other aspects of college sports. Recruiting is one of those aspects. College athlete recruitment is particularly thorny, as the process necessarily involves interaction with a talent pool in which many members are not legally able to enter into contracts. Nonetheless, a process needs to be established whereby commitments are honored on both sides of the table. This will be an important role for the NCAA and one that also necessitates legislation at the federal level to back the NCAA up.

Transfer regulations will also be a critical area for the NCAA to address. Similar to the U.S. economy, it should be desired that a free market be in existence for talent in intercollegiate athletics, with the understanding that transfers are disruptive both to student athletes and programs. Policies and procedures need to be enshrined to avoid the transfer process turning into a free-for-all while nonetheless providing athletes and member institutions with options to participate in a fair and orderly secondary market for player positions.

Conduct is another very critical area of college sports that is in need of additional regulation. Recent anecdotal observation provides evidence of a lack of enforcement of conduct violation. This is not surprising given the fact that the NCAA, having been disintermediated from much of the revenue generated by college athletics, lacks the power to enforce its own rules. Many times, it is incumbent to the conference or member institution to enforce conduct codes. Unfortunately, this oftentimes presents a conflict of interest.

In other areas where the NCAA has attempted to legislate and govern intercollegiate athletics, it may make more sense to simplify the rules. For too long, the NCAA rule book was a wasp's nest of counterintuitive regulations that were nearly impossible to enforce. In a situation where the NCAA is the undisputed governing authority in college sports, a simpler regulatory framework will facilitate both compliance and enforcement.

Beyond antitrust, federal legislation will be required to address the labor issue that has been making its way through the courts. Many states have passed legislation, frequently bipartisan, that has made it clear that student athletes are not employees of their member institutions. This is an important distinction for many aforementioned reasons. In order for college athletics to remain in the manifestation that we currently enjoy, players will need to persist as independent contractors.

In a recent development, a U.S. Appeals Court in Philadelphia ruled in June 2024 that certain college athletes *may* be considered employees if their efforts primarily benefit their schools.[14] The Appeals Court suggested a test for whether athletes' efforts on behalf of their respective programs constitute recreation or labor.[14] U.S. Circuit Judge L. Felipe Restrepo stated, "Ultimately, the touchstone remains whether the cumulative circumstances of the relationship between the athlete and college or NCAA reveal an economic reality that is that of an employee-employer."[14] Following this ruling, the case will be returned to the original trial judge, an outcome unfavorable to the NCAA, which had hoped to have the action dismissed.

The cryptic nature of the ruling, and its avoidance of the question, are instructive of the need for legislation to finally decide this issue. Especially with the advent of NIL, most of the economic value of college athletes is generated away from the member institutions. Therefore, a structure that considers them employees runs counter to the direction of the flow of funds. Once this is codified into law, a significant amount of uncertainty surrounding the future of intercollegiate athletics will be resolved.

In June of 2024, around the same time of the Protect the Ball Act, HR 8534, known as "The Protecting Student Athletes' Economic Freedom Act," was introduced.[15] The law would definitively determine that college athletes are not employees of their educational institutions under any state or federal law, including the NLRA, which has heretofore empowered the NLRB to involve itself in this issue.[15] Default independent contractor status for student athletes would extend to all institutions of higher education, as well as conferences and athletic associations.[15]

On June 13, the U.S. House of Representatives Education and Workforce Committee held a hearing on the bill and advanced it by a vote of 23-16 for consideration by the broader House.[15] The measure advanced along party lines, with Representative Bob Good (R-VA), the bill's sponsor, stating that employment relationships represent an "existential threat" to intercollegiate athletics.[15] Conversely, Democratic Representative Bobby Scott (D-VA) reacted that the bill "strips varsity athletes from their rights under fundamental labor and employment statutes."[15]

While the labor issue has become a partisan debate, hopefully as senators and congressman come to realize that unionizing college sports will herald the destruction of the industry, there can be a reconciliation of the viewpoints involved. In the absence of transparent legislation at the federal level, the issue will be left in the interim to the courts. Given the impact that this issue will have on U.S. society, the proper medium for its resolution is with elected representatives, not appointed judges.

For the college sports industry to remain viable, there will need to be a resolution at the federal level to both the antitrust and the labor issue. This is no small feat for a Congress that is known more for gridlock than dual pronged initiatives. As such, it would likely make sense for some of the legislation that has already been introduced to be combined into a comprehensive package that addresses all of these substantial maladies that are confronting intercollegiate athletics.

In this process, it will be important for the public to be supportive of legislative efforts taken on behalf of the NCAA and other organizations involved in the promotion of college sports that seek to stem the tide of antitrust litigation and labor unionization. This is one of the reasons that I authored this book—to enlighten people to the accounting and financial impact that will become more apparent as this discussion advances. Hopefully, this helps pave the way for sound policy that will preserve an important U.S. institution.

Key takeaways from this chapter include:

1. The industry of intercollegiate athletics currently faces a dual threat from vociferous antitrust litigation, as well as attempts to unionize or otherwise create an employer–employee relationship between players and schools.
2. Federal legislation, which is necessary for definitively resolving these threats, has been proposed in numerous forms in both houses of Congress.
3. The success of legislative efforts to provide for antitrust exemption/protection for the NCAA, and define college athletes intractably as independent contractors, will be required to ensure that the industry of college sports remains an extant part of our society.

14

Conclusion

At the beginning of this book, we discussed that income taxes were prohibited under the original U.S. Constitution as a direct tax that needed to be apportioned among the states, such that the tax per person was equivalent. This concept of apportionment, while obsolete from authoritative perspective in the tax code, is nonetheless relevant to industries that would be disproportionately impacted by inadequate tax strategies. Intercollegiate athletics is one of those industries and, as such, it is important for its principal participants to be cognizant of the tax consequences of recent developments.

The 16th amendment emerged out of the necessity to finance a war — World War I to be exact. While this was a conflict that the United States was only briefly involved in, it was transformative for Europe and marked a watershed event in American tax policy as the amendment passed to pay for it expressly permitted direct taxation without apportionment. It was, regardless, an inevitable event as less than two decades later, Europe was embroiled in another conflagration that the United States would play a leading role in. Our success in World War II is due in no small part to the size of our economy and by extension the government's ability to directly tax it to fuel the war effort. As such, taxes do have a positive impact on society when directed in the right manner.

In 1939, directly prior to WWII, the various laws and statutes pertaining to federal taxation were summarily codified. A more comprehensive codification, that reads similarly to the modern code, was established in 1954. It would undergo substantive revision in 1986 forming the Tax Code of 1986 which is considered the modern tax code. Certain adjustments made in between the 1954 and the 1986 codes are relevant to this discussion, as are some stipulations of the Tax Cuts and Jobs Act of 2017. Suffice it to say, major revisions to the U.S. tax code have been few and far between and the purpose of this book is to advocate for sound policy that operates within the existing tax laws rather than make any changes to the Code.

Important to analyzing the current Code are its stipulations on exempt organizations. The 1954 IRC introduced Section 501(c)(3) and it explicitly lists entities formed for educational purposes as exempt from corporate income taxes and further schedules them in Section 170 as eligible to accept charitable contributions.

Educational purpose has been the most oft cited reason for exemption for college sports in IRS publications. Maintaining educational value is therefore key for college sports to retain charitable distinction under the Code.

Inextricably linked to the educational value of college sports is its secondary exemption granted by the Tax Reform Act of 1976 which intersected the IRCs of 1954 and 1986. Driven by Cold War international competition, the TRA exempts organizations that foster amateur sports competition. Intended to capitalize the training of Olympic athletes, the Act had the collateral impact of providing another avenue of charitable qualification for college athletics. Rather than mutually exclusive, however, the educational value and "amateur" status of college sports are inseverable and these exemptions need to be thought of in concert with one another.

This is especially the case given the storied history of college sports. Emerging from the ebbed tide of Puritanism and driven by an envy of British athleticism, the institution was mildly controversial from the start. As the early nineteenth century had already ushered in the Industrial Revolution, this could be seen as a nostalgic return to the ideals of an agricultural aristocracy.

Added to this was the influence of the Civil War on the development of college athletics, especially football, in the South. Described as a "war game" the sport was sometimes seen as a proxy for battlefield combat. Not surprisingly, early football was a somewhat dangerous activity.

Rising injuries and even deaths led to calls for reform in the early twentieth century. President Theodore Roosevelt himself led the cause for reform. Ultimately, the IAUS, which eventually became the NCAA, was created to regulate the burgeoning industry.

From the 1800s, schools had been organizing themselves into conferences and this continued as the 20th century progressed. Regional organizations sponsored events featuring local favorite teams. Some of these were one-off or short lived while others ultimately morphed into the modern day Bowl games.

The mid part of the 1900s saw the advent of scandals in college athletics. Mainly involving basketball and typically including a combination of kickbacks, gambling and organized crime, these sordid occurrences left an indelible scar on the institutions entangled in them and college sports as a whole. These headlines offer a lesson to be heeded especially as online sports betting is gaining wider acceptance.

Intercollegiate athletics would experience future scandals certain of which threatened academic integrity and others of which involved violent and lascivious criminal behavior. Conference realignments continue to grab fan attention to this day. Amidst all of this, it is all the more important for college sports to keep sight of its educational purpose.

An unfortunate distraction from this purpose has been precipitated by an early 20th century invention that has captivated the population. Following the advent of television, the FCC's regulatory apparatus paved the way for athletics in general to dominate the medium due to its independent and salubrious content. Unfortunately, this became the genesis of the problem as contention over broadcast games put the NCAA at odds with certain of its member institutions and their conferences. Ultimately this led to the landmark antitrust settlement of 1984 in *NCAA v. Board of Regents of University of Oklahoma* that undermined the NCAA's role as an overriding regulator of college sports and disintermediated it from the majority of football broadcast revenue. Today, the Power 5 conferences generate billions in revenue from broadcast rights all of which is shielded from federal taxation by the dual exemptions intercollegiate athletics enjoys for its contribution to the educational mission of the member institutions and its fostering of amateur athletics.

In the absence of these exemptions, the concept of UBTI would apply. UBTI provides for taxation of income earned by otherwise exempt entities for activities that do not contribute importantly to their charitable purpose. The criteria for UBTI include revenues earned from operations that are 1) are derived from a trade or business; 2) are regularly carried on; and 3) are not substantially related to the entity's exempt purpose. College sports easily meets the first two criteria while there has been some debate about the third. Intercollegiate athletics have been determined in past IRS revenue rulings to be substantially related to their host institutions' charitable educational purpose as a college or university. This, however, occurred in prior manifestations of the industry which were not as extensive in size of revenue as they are today. In addition, such findings pre-date an important regulatory fiat in the form of Treasury Regulation 1.513 which would impose UBTI on activities that are conducted on a larger scale than necessary to further an exempt purpose. It is highly likely that college sports, especially in a professionalized model, would be considered under this regulation to be disproportionate to the educational purpose of the member instituions. Therefore, the industry needs to avail itself of both exemptions, education and nonprofessionalism, to remain tax free.

Over time, the concept of amateurism has been equated with a purist definition that more closely relates to volunteerism. This likely comes from the infatuation with the British aristocracy that originally drove the development of college sports where it was considered dishonorable to receive any compensation for engaging in sport. In the United States, this strictly defined amateurism never existed as players were receiving compensation in some shape or form from the very beginning. Rather, what has prevailed and what should continue to be practiced is what this book terms *nonprofessionalism*.

Through legislation, specifically the Stevens Act, the United States government has essentially delegated the determination of amateur status to international Olympic governing bodies. Today, this determination allows for a broad range of compensation arrangements for Olympic athletes that do not void their status as amateur Olympians. If college sports can successfully follow the Olympic model, it will be able to retain non-professional status as it relates to the Tax Code and will continue to enjoy its dual exemptions from federal taxation.

In this way, recent developments in the world of NIL do not necessitate a departure from the non-professional model of college sports which preserves its tax exemption. In fact, NIL is actually beneficial in that it further distinguishes college athletes as independent of their member institutions as it concerns any theorized employee-employer relationship. Regulation of these arrangements will be important to ensure they are free of corrupting influences to avoid a repeat of the scandals of previous decades involving a host of bad actors. The IRS has made it clear that NIL collectives, which have sprung up at member institutions across the country with some multiple collectives associated with certain schools, do not qualify for charitable exemption. It should be the role of the NCAA to determine how these collectives operate. This will be critical to preserving the benefits that NIL provides without it distracting from or undermining the educational purpose of the industry. These benefits of NIL include the positive impact of attracting new forms of capital to the industry from private investors and propelling women's sports into increasing popularity.

On the downside, recent NIL developments unfortunately catalyzed litigation related to foregone compensation from prior periods when NIL was disallowed. Added to a number of other complaints against the NCAA, these suits led to the May 2024 landmark settlement whereby the NCAA and the conferences will earmark up to 22 percent of inflows for revenue sharing. Combined with changes to the transfer portal that substantially ease restrictions on mobility between programs, this has ushered in a new era for the industry. While the settlement does not immediately impact the tax status of college athletics, the manner in which it is discharged will have wide-ranging implications for the business model going forward. It is important that revenue sharing preserve the independent contractor status of the players and transfer regulations should be imposed to prevent wholesale disruption to the functioning of teams and recruiting programs.

This leads to a key issue confronting college sports today—the labor issue. Certain parties, aided by one or more officials from the NLRB, have asserted that college athletes should properly be categorized as employees of the institutions they play for. In addition, as employees they would have the right to unionize and engage in collective bargaining with their member institutions. While this is being actively resisted by the

NCAA, the conferences and the schools themselves, it would have substantial negative impact if it ever materialized. An employer-employee relationship would fully professionalize the industry and thereby nullify both of the charitable exemptions it enjoys for its important contribution to education and the incubation of amateur athletics.

As shown in this book, the financial cost of such an event would be catastrophic. Not only would it expose institutions, conferences and the NCAA to taxes in the form of UBTI at the federal and potentially state level, it would enjoin the industry from a significant source of revenue in the form of charitable contributions that would no longer be tax deductible. In addition, it is unlikely the professionalized sports could continue to avail themselves of support from the institution's tuition revenue or state taxpayer resources given the likely public outcry against such appropriations. Suffice it to say, the concept of college athletics would cease to exist in its current form. Moreover, given the strength of professional sports, it is unlikely college athletics would fare well if it became a direct competitor to for-profit sports leagues like the NFL, NBA, MLB, NHL and others. What college athletics would ultimately look like is uncertain, but it should be well known in advance that it will be a deadweight loss to American society.

The motivation behind advocation for this path is unclear but it may stem from the origins of college athletics as a means to emulate the British Empire. Given the negativity associated with international empires in general, colonialism and the rigid class system employed in Great Britain, some of this ill sentiment may have attached itself to college sports. A more likely motivator has been the well-publicized anti college football movement which cites the dangers of the sport and its distraction from academics as reasons for it to be banned in the United States. Also, recent studies have shown that Gen Z is less interested in sports broadly than prior generations and that a material percentage of them actually consider themselves to be "anti-sport."

Whatever inspires detractors of college sports, it is important for us not to go down the destructive path charted by these parties but rather employ sound policy to address recent developments in the industry. Federal legislation will be needed to put the decision in the hands of elected officials versus court judges and labor boards that are not voted on by the public. Some form of antitrust exemption, similar to the one enjoyed by MLB, will be needed to allow the NCAA to function as an overriding regulator for college sports without attracting voluminous litigation. In addition, it will be important for Congress to make it clear that college athletes are not employees of their member institutions but rather independent contractors. In this way, college sports will be able to retain their charitable exempt status and rules and regulations can be effectively enforced to ensure that this great American institution can continue to entertain and educate future generations of U.S. citizens.

Key takeaways from this book:

1. College athletics has enjoyed a rich history stretching back to the late nineteenth century. This author believes that it should continue to persist in substantially its same format for decades to come.

2. Recent developments in the industry of college sports, especially regarding the labor issue, have put it on a collision course with its charitable tax exempt status. The financial consequences of college sports losing its dual exemptions would be disastrous and need to be avoided by all means necessary.

3. Sound policy at the federal level through Congressional legislation is needed to cement the NCAA's role as the overriding regulator of college sports and to solidify college athletes' status as independent contractors. In this way, the industry will be able to maintain its charitable tax exempt status and continue to prosper.

About the Author

Thomas A. McGovern is a Certified Public Accountant (CPA) and holds the Chartered Financial Analyst (CFA) designation. His extensive career includes twenty years as a Wall Street investment banker and equity research analyst. He has been involved in the higher education sector as a member of the board of directors of the University of Virginia's Manhattan alumni group, the Virginia Club of New York, and President of the Board of Governors of the St. Elmos national organization. Thomas McGovern earned a Master of Business Administration (MBA) from the Darden Graduate School of Business at the University of Virginia and an AB in Economics from Hamilton College where he graduated summa cum laude.

References

Chapter 1

1. U.S. Census Bureau 2. Internal Revenue Service 3. National Archives 4. U.S. Senate 5. U.S. Government Publishing Office 6. House.gov

Chapter 2

1. Independent Sector 2. IRS Tax Based Research 3. Nonprofit Charitable Organizations 1986 and 1987 4. Internal Revenue Code of 1954 5. Olympics. com 6. Joint Committee on Taxation 7. IRS "Amateur Athletic Organizations" working paper

Chapter 3

1. William & Mary; Harvard University 2. Britannica 3. Lewis, Guy. The Beginnings of Organized Collegiate Sport 4. History of the SEC Conference. 5. Big 10 6. ncaa.org 7. FBSchedules 8. Missouri Valley Conference 9. The PAC 12 10. Census.gov 11. Britannica 12. NAIA 13. NAIA By the Numbers 14. NCAA History of the Tournament 15. History.com 16. SI Vault 17. Sportsrec.com 18. NYU Local 19. Sports History Weekly; Goldstein, Joe. Explosion: 1951 scandal threatens college hoops.; Bray, Tyler. The History of NYU Basketball You Didn't Know 20. The Wall Street Journal 21. Purdum, David. The Worst Fix Ever. ESPN. 22. PrepScholar. 23. SI Vault 24. The Big East Conference 25. Whittington, Samantha. "The Madness" of Basketball Related IP. Suiter Swantz 26. Wilco, Daniel. NCAA.com 27. Associated Press 28. Wikipedia 29. College Football Playoff 30. Carolina Alumni Review 31. Reuters 32. ESPN

Chapter 4

1. Britannica 2. Mitel: "The History of the Federal Communications Commission" 3. PBS.com "Nixon's Checkers Speech" 4. Statista 5. Federal Communications Commission (FCC) 6. Federal Trade Commission (FTC) 7. Fast Company 8. National Archives 9. NCAA v. Board of Regents of University of Oklahoma, 468 U.S. 85 (1984) 10. USA Today 11. WSJ 12. CBS Sports; Fox Sports 13. Conference websites 14. Knight-Newhouse College Athletics Database

Chapter 5

1. Internal Revenue Service (IRS) 2. Arnsberg, Ludlum, Riley, & Stanton "A History of the Tax Exempt Sector: An SOI Perspective" 3. Internal Revenue Code 4. UNC Law 5. RR 80-296, 1980-2, C.B. 195

Chapter 6

1. Britannica 2. NCAA 3. Merriam Webster Dictionary 4. Supreme Court of the United States 5. USGA 6. USTA 7. Olympics.com 8. The Economist 9. The United States Olympic & Paralympic Committee (USOPC) 10. International Olympic Committee (IOC)

Chapter 7

1. Sportico 2. Foster Swift Collins & Smith 3. Baker Tilly 4. NCAA 5. University of Virginia Athletics 6. The Oklahoman 7. University of Texas Athletics 8. University of Missouri Athletics 9. Saul Ewing 10. On3 11. International Olympic Committee (IOC) 12. Olympic Broadcasting Services (OBS) 13. Internal Revenue Service 14. Wall Street Journal

Chapter 8

1. Associated Press 2. Grant vs. NCAA 3. Commonwealth of Virginia and the State of Tennessee vs. NCAA 4. Associated Press – Injunction Granted 5. Carter vs. NCAA 6. Fontenot vs. NCAA 7. Hubbard vs. NCAA 8. Brantmeier v NCAA 9. Members of the NC State 1983 Men's Basketball National Championship Team v. the NCAA 10. United States Department of Justice 11. Various States vs. NCAA 12. NCAA 13. Raleigh Observer 14. Riley Gaines et. al v. NCAA et al. 15. Hagens Berman and Winston & Strawn Joint Settlement Statement 16. Ropes & Gray

Chapter 9

1. BBC Dartmouth's Men's Basketball 2. Associated Press 3. NLRB 4. Northwestern University and College Athletes Players Association (CAPA), petitioner 5. Internal Revenue Service 6. National Archives 7. Deloitte 8. Department of Labor FLSA 9. Department of Labor 10. IRS full time student

Chapter 10

1. IRS Revenue Ruling 80-296 2. IRS UBTI Technical Guide 3. IRS Office of Chief Counsel Memorandum AM 2023-004 4. Merriam-Webster Dictionary. Note: Reference materials consulted include those produced by Becker Professional Education Corporation.

Chapter 11

1. Tax Foundation 2. U.S. News & World Report 3. NBA G-League 4. Pro Football Network 5. The Knight-Newhouse College Athletics Database 6. Statista 7. Statista & Infoplease 8. NCAA

Chapter 12

1. Britannica 2. NY Times archives 3. Inside Higher Education 4. Wikipedia 5. The Eagle 6. Creighton University 7. Arkansas Democrat Gazette 8. Bostonia 9. BU Today 10. ESPN 11. The Philadelphia Inquirer 12. Wall Street Journal 13. Iona University Athletics 14. The Core 15. Forbes 16. USA Today 17. The Diplomat 18. SportEdge

Chapter 13

1. National Archives 2. The Federal Trade Commission 3. Associated Press 4. Gwartney, James D. Stroup, Richard L. Sobel, Russell S. "Economics: Private and Public Choice." Dryden Press. 5. North Carolina Utilities Commission 6. The Surface Transportation Board 7. The Federal Railway Administration 8. National Constitution Center 9. Congress.gov 10. USA Today 11. NCAA 12. ESPN 13. Federal Election Commission 14. Fox Sports 15. National Legal Review

Bibliography

Chapter 1

Internal Revenue Service. *Historical Highlights of the IRS*. Last updated September 13, 2024. Extracted 11.03.2024. www.irs.gov

U.S. National Archives and Records Administration. *16ᵗʰ Amendment to the U.S. Constitution: Federal Income Tax (1913)*. Extracted 11.03.2024. www.archives.gov

United States Census Bureau. *Title 26, U.S. Code*. Last revised August 3, 2023. Extracted 1.05.2025. www.census.gov

United States House of Representatives. *Title 26 – Internal Revenue Code*. August 16, 1954, October 22, 1986. www.house.gov

United States Senate. *Revenue Act of 1939*. June 21, 1939. www.senate.gov

United States. Government Publishing Office. *Internal Revenue Code of 1954*. January 6, 1954. Extracted 7.23.2023. www.gpo.gov

Chapter 2

Hilgert, Cecilia and Maher, Susan J. *Nonprofit Charitable Organizations, 1986 and 1987*. Internal Revenue Service. Extracted 10.01.2023. www.irs.gov

Independent Sector. *Health of the U.S. Nonprofit Sector*. November 2023. Extracted 10.13.2024. www.independentsector.org

Internal Revenue Service. *Amateur Athletic Organizations*. Derived from 1980 EO CPE text. Extracted 12.03.2023. www.irs.gov

Joint Committee on Taxation. *General Explanation of the Tax Reform Act of 1976*. December 29, 1976. Extracted 1.05.2025. www.jct.gov

Skelly, Daniel F. *Tax-Based Research and Data on Nonprofit Organizations, 1975-1990*. Internal Revenue Service. Extracted 10.13.2024. www.irs.gov

The Olympic Games. *Montreal 1976: Overview; Results: Medal Table*. Extracted 1.05.2025. Olympics.com

United States Government Publishing Office. *Internal Revenue Code of 1954*. January 6, 1954. Extracted 7.23.2023 www.gpo.gov

Chapter 3

Big 10 Conference. *About the Conference*. Extracted 1.16.2024. https://bigten.org

Big East Conference. *The Big East Conference History*. Extracted 3.10.2024. www.bigeast.com

Bray, Tyler. *The History of NYU Basketball You Didn't Know*. NYU Local. November 13, 2014. Extracted 2.25.2024. https://nyulocal.com

Britannica. *ACC Conference History*. Extracted 3.10.2024. www.britannica.com

Britannica. *Big 10 Conference History*. Extracted 3.10.2024. www.brtiannica.com

Britannica. *Big 12 Conference History*. Extracted 3.10.2024. www.britannica.com

Britannica. *Early Universities*. Extracted 10.28.2024. www.britannica.com

Cacciola, Scott. *NYU Holds Out on Sports*. The Wall Street Journal. Updated May 1, 2010. Extracted 2.25.2024. www.wsj.com

Carolina Alumni Review. *SACS Restores UNC to Full Accreditation*. June 16, 2016. Extracted 3.17.2024. https://alumni.unc.edu

College Football Playoff. *Bowl Championship Series (BCS) All-Time Results*. Extracted 1.15.2024 https://collegefootballplayoff.com

College Football Playoff. *Overview*. Extracted 3.03.2024. https://collegefootball-playoff.com

Daughters, Amy. *Tracking the Growth in College Football Bowl Games*. April 8, 2015. FBS Schedules. Extracted 1.15.2024. https://fbschedules.com

Einstein, Charles. *When Football Went to War*. December 6, 1971. SI Vault. Extracted 1.05.2025. https://vault.si.com

Fisk, Judy. *Sports in America in the 1950s*. SportsRec. April 16, 2011. Extracted 1.08.2024. www.sportsrec.com

Goldstein, Joe. *Explosion: 1951 Scandal Threatens College Hoops*. Sports History Weekly

Harvard University. www.harvard.edu

Herskovitz, Jon. *Baylor University Faces U.S. Probe Over Response to Sex Assaults*. October 20, 2016. Reuters. Extracted 3.13.2024. www.reuters.com

Klein, Christopher. *How Military Service Teams Dominated College Football During World War II*. Updated November 21, 2021. Extracted 1.05.2025. www.history.com

Lewis, Guy. *The Beginnings of Organized Collegiate Sport*. Johns Hopkins University Press. Extracted 1.07.2024. www.jstor.org

Missouri Valley Conference. https://mvc-sports.com

National Association of Intercollegiate Athletics. *NAIA by the Numbers.* Extracted 6.02.2024. www.naia.org

National Association of Intercollegiate Athletics. *NAIA History.* Extracted 6.02.2024. www.naia.org

National Collegiate Athletic Association. *History: BCS Championship.* December 19, 2013. Extracted 2.25.2024. www.ncaa.com

National Collegiate Athletic Association. *Men's Basketball Championship History.* Extracted 1.15.2024. www.ncaa.com

National Collegiate Athletic Association. *Timeline.* Extracted 3.03.2024. www. ncaa.org

Pac-12 Conference. *History of the Pac-12 Conference.* Extracted 1.16.2024. https:// pac-12.com

PrepScholar. *What Are NCAA Divisions? Division 1 vs 2 vs 3.* Extracted 3.03.2024. www.prepscholar.com

Purdum, David. *The Worst Fix Ever.* ESPN. October 3, 2014. Extracted 1.15.2024. www.espn.com

Reynolds, Tim. *AP Source: NBA, Union Forward Talks on Ending 'One-and-Done'.* February 21, 2019. Associated Press. Extracted 3.12.2024. https://apnews.com

Southeastern Conference. *History of the Southeastern Conference.* Extracted 1.15.2024. www.secsports.com

Sports History Weekly. *Corruption Mars College Basketball in New York.* March 26, 2023. Extracted 2.11.2024. www.sportshistoryweekly.com

Underwood, John. *The NCAA Splits its Decision.* SI Vault. Extracted 3.02.2024. https://vault.si.com

United States Census. *History: September 2023. U.S. Census Bureau History: Philo Farnsworth and the Invention of Television.* Extracted 1.08.2024. www. census.gov

Whittington, Samantha. *"The Madness" of Basketball Related IP.* March 15, 2023. Suiter Swantz IP. Extracted 1.15.2024. https://suiter.com

Wikipedia. *Penn State Child Sex Abuse Scandal.* Extracted 1.05.2025. https:// en.wikipedia.org

Wilco, Daniel. *March Madness History: A Comprehensive Guide to the Men's Tournament*. March 23, 2023. National Collegiate Athletic Association. Extracted 1.15.2024. www.ncaa.com

William & Mary. *History and Traditions*. Extracted 10.13.2024. www.wm.edu

Chapter 4

Bachman, Rachel and Simoneti, Isabella. *NCAA Women Beat Men in Ratings, Not TV Pay*. April 10, 2024. The Wall Street Journal. Extracted 4.10.2024. www.wsj.com

Berkowitz, Steve. *NCAA Recorded Nearly $1.3 Billion in Revenue in 2023, Putting Net Assets at $565 Million*. February 1, 2024. USA Today. Extracted 8.18.2024. www.usatoday.com

Britannica. *American Broadcasting Company*. Extracted 4.01.2024. www.britannica.com

Britannica. *The Era of Television*. Extracted 3.17.2024. www.britannica.com

Britannica. *Television in the United States*. Extracted 3.17.2024. www.britannica.com

Fast Company. *How the Supreme Court Broke the NCAA's Lock on TV Revenue*. March 3, 2024. Extracted 4/7/2024. www.fastcompany.com

Federal Communications Commission. *The Policy and Regulatory Landscape*. Extracted 4.03.2024. www.fcc.gov

Federal Trade Commission. *Evaluation of the Syndication and Financial Interest Rules*. September 5, 1990

Fox Sports. *Big Ten, SEC Are Top Conferences in Revenue with Athlete Pay on the Horizon*. Published May 24, 2024. Extracted 1.02.2025. www.foxsports.com

Knight-Newhouse College Athletics Database. *Football Bowl Subdivision: Where the Money Goes*. 2023. Knight Commission on Intercollegiate Athletics and Syracuse University Newhouse School of Public Communications. Extracted 1.05.2025. https://knightnewnousedata.org

Mitel. *History of the Federal Communications Commission*. n.d. www.mitel.com

National Archives. *Sherman Anti-Trust Act*. July 2, 1890. Extracted 4.07.2024. www.archives.gov

PBS Charlotte. *Nixon's Checkers Speech*. Extracted 10.14.2023. www.wtvi.org

Statista. *Revenue of the NCAA from Television Broadcast Payments and Licensing Rights from 2012-2027.* Extracted 3.17.2024. www.statista.com

Statista. *Average Revenue Per Employee of Professional Services Organizations.* Extracted 4.11.2024. www.statista.com

Strake, Dean. *Big Ten Leads Power Five Conferences with $854.6 Million in Revenue in 2022 Fiscal Year, Per Report.* May 19, 2023. CBS Sports. Extracted 3.17.2024. www.cbssports.com

United States Supreme Court. *NCAA v. Board of Regents of University of Oklahoma, 468 U.S. 85 (1984).* Decided June 2, 1984. Justia. Extracted 4.07.2024. www.justia.com

Chapter 5

Arnsberger, Paul and Ludlum, Melissa. Riley, Margaret. Stanton, Mark. *A History of the Tax-Exempt Sector: An SOI Perspective.* Winter 2008. Internal Revenue Service. Extracted 4.14.2024. www.irs.gov

Internal Revenue Service. *Exempt Organizations Technical Guide: TG 48: Unrelated Business Income Tax.* Revision date 12/15/2023. Extracted 4.14.2024. www.irs.gov

Internal Revenue Service. *Revenue Ruling 80-296, 1980-2, C.B. 195.* Extracted 5.05.2024. www.irs.gov

Lowndes, Charles L. *The Revenue Act of 1950.* UNC School of Law: North Carolina Law Review. Volume 39. Number 2. Extracted 4.14.2024. http://scholarship.law.unc.edu/nclr/vol29/iss2/1

U.S. House of Representatives. *Revenue Act of 1950.* September 21, 1950. Extracted 4.14.2024. www.house.gov

Chapter 6

Britannica. *Scholarships and The Student Athlete.* Extracted 5.06.2024. www.britannica.com

International Olympic Committee. *Commercial Opportunities for Participants During the Olympic Games Paris 2024.* Extracted 5.30.2024. www.olympics.com

Merriam Webster Dictionary. *Various.* Extracted 5.06.2024; 5.07.2024; 5.15.2024. www.merriam-webster.com

National Collegiate Athletic Association. *History.* Extracted 5.06.2024. www.ncaa.org

National Collegiate Athletic Association. *NCAA Graduation Rates: A Quarter-Century of Tracking Academic Success.* Extracted 5.16.2024. www.ncaa.org

Olympics.com. *List of Olympic Sports.* Extracted 5.12.2024. www.olympics.com

Supreme Court of the United States. *National Collegiate Athletic Association v. Alston et al.* Decided June 21, 2021. Extracted 10.17.2024. www.supremecourt.gov

The Economist. *Why Did The Olympics Ditch Their Amateur-Athlete Requirement?* July 20,2021. Extracted 5.19.2024. www.economist.com

United States Golf Association. *Rules of Amateur Status FAQs.* Extracted 5.19.2024. www.usga.org

United States Olympic & Paralympic Committee. *Bylaws of the United States Olympic & Paralympic Committee.* Effective as of April 1, 2024. Extracted 5.22.2024. www.usopc.org

United States Olympic & Paralympic Committee. *History: About the U.S. Olympic & Paralympic Leadership.* Extracted 5.22.2024. www.usopc.org

United States Tennis Association. *Eligibility Rules and Guidelines.* Extracted 5.19.2024. www.usta.com

Chapter 7

Andrews, Kaitlyn. *Institutions Begin Paying Student Athletes Following Alston Ruling.* December 1, 2021. Baker Tilly. Extracted 6.02.2024. www.bakertilly.com

Beaton, Andrew and Radnofsky, Louise. *College Sports is About to Turn Pro. Private Equity Wants In.* May 22, 2024. The Wall Street Journal. Extracted 6.04.2024. www.wsj.com

Camillo, Lynne A. *Office of Chief Counsel Memorandum: Whether Operation of an NIL Collective Furthers an Exempt Purpose Under Section 501(c)(3).* Released June 9, 2023. Internal Revenue Service. Extracted 6.03.2024. www.irs.gov

Dalimonte, Anthony. *NIL Timeline: The Events that Transformed College Sports.* April 21, 2023. Foster Swift Collins & Smith P.C. Extracted 6.02.2024. www.fosterswift.com

Hosick, Michelle Brutlag. *NCAA Adopts Interim Name, Image and Likeness Policy.* June 30, 2021. National Collegiate Athletic Association. Extracted 6.02.2024. www.ncaa.org

International Olympic Committee. https://olympics.com

McCann, Michael. *Ed O'Bannon Stands Tall Over NCAA Antitrust Settlement.* May 29, 2024. Sportico. Extracted 6.02.2024. www.sportico.com

Olympic Broadcasting Services. www.obs.tvCamillo, Lynne A. *Office of Chief Counsel Memorandum: Whether Operation of an NIL Collective Furthers an Exempt Purpose Under Section 501(c)(3).* Released June 9, 2023. Internal Revenue Service. Extracted 6.03.2024. www.irs.gov

On3. *NIL Collectives.* Extracted 10.20.2024. www.on3.com

Saul Ewing. *NIL Legislation Tracker.* Extracted 10.21.2024. www.saul.com

Sulley, Colton. *Gov. Stitt Signs Bill on Name, Image and Likeness. Here's what it means for OU, OSU.* April 24, 2024. The Oklahoman. Extracted 6.02.2024. www.oklahoman.com

University of Missouri Athletics. *Mizzou Athletics Continues NIL Evolution.* July 7, 2023. Extracted 6.04.2024. https://mutigers.com

University of Texas Athletics. *Texas Name, Image, Likeness (NIL) Law Summary.* Effective July 1, 2023. Extracted 6.04.2024. https://texaslonghorns.com

White, Jeff. *NIL Bill to Be Impactful For UVA Athletics.* April 10, 2024. Virginia Athletics. Extracted 6.02.2024. www.virginiasports.com

Chapter 8

Alexander, Chip and Pelletier, Justin. *UNC Football Receiver Tez Walker Granted Immediate NCAA Eligibility. Here's Why.* Updated October 6, 2023. Raleigh Observer. Extracted 6.09.2024. www.newsobserver.com

Associated Press. *How Many Legal Challenges is the NCAA Facing? It is A Lot and the Impacts Could be Big.* Updated March 5, 2024. Extracted 6.08.2024. https://apnews.com

Burnsed, Brian. *St. Bonaventure's Road to* Redemption. March 28, 2012. National Collegiate Athletic Association. Extracted 6.09.2024. www.ncaa.org

Conniff, Christopher P.; Coleman, Dennis M.; Han, Erica L.; Young, David; Freshman, Daniel; Wheeler, Tatum; Myers, Kennedy and Gondalia Parv. *NCAA and Power Five Conferences Agree to $2.8 Billion Proposed Settlement of Antitrust Litigation.* May 30, 2024. Ropes & Gray. Extracted 6.08.2024. www.ropesgray.com

Hagens Berman and Winston & Strawn. *Hagens Berman and Winston & Strawn Secure Historic Multibillion-Dollar Settlement for College Athletes and Bring*

Revolutionary Change to College Sports. May 23, 2024. Extracted 6.10.2024. www.hbsslaw and www.winston.com

State of North Carolina, In the General Court of Justice, Superior Court Division, County of Wake. *Members of North Carolina State University's 1983 Men's Basketball National Championship Team v. National Collegiate Athletic Association and Collegiate Licensing Company.* Filed June 2024

United States Department of Justice. *Justice Department Joins Lawsuit Challenging National Collegiate Athletic Association's (NCAA) Transfer Eligibility Rule.* January 18, 2024. Office of Public Affairs. Extracted 6.09.2024. www.justice.gov

United States District Court, District of Colorado. *Alex Fontenot v. National Collegiate Athletic Association et. al.* Filed November 20, 2023

United States District Court, Eastern District of Tennessee, Knoxville Division. *State of Tennessee and Commonwealth of Virginia v. National Collegiate Athletic Association.* Filed February 23, 2024

United States District Court, Middle District of North Carolina. *Reese Brantmeier v. National Collegiate Athletic Association.* Filed March 18, 2024

United States District Court, Northern District of California, Oakland Division. *Grant House and Sedona Prince v. National Collegiate Athletic Association et al.* Filed June 15, 2020

United States District Court, Northern District of California, Oakland Division. *Chuba Hubbard and Keira McCarrell v. National Collegiate Athletic Association et. al.* Filed April 4, 2023

United States District Court, Northern District of Georgia, Atlanta Division. *Riley Gaines et al. v. National Collegiate Athletic Association et. al.* Filed March 14, 2024

United States District Court, Northern District of West Virginia, Clarksburg Division. *Various States and United States of America, U.S. Department of Justice et al. v. National Collegiate Athletic Association.* Filed January 18, 2024

United States Judicial Panel on Multidistrict Litigation. *In Re College Athlete Compensation Antitrust Litigation, Brief in Support of Plaintiff's Motion for Transfer of Actions to the Northern District of California Pursuant to 28 U.S.C. S 1407 for Coordinated or Consolidated Pretrial Procedures.* Filed January 16, 2024

Walker, Teresa M. and Russo, Ralph D. *Judge Hands NCAA Another Loss, Says Compensation Rules Likely Violate Antitrust Law, Harm Athletes.* Updated February 23, 2024. Associated Press. Extracted 6.09.2024. https://apnews.com

Chapter 9

Associated Press. *Dartmouth Refuses to Work with Basketball Player's Union, Potentially Sending Case to Federal Court.* Updated March 18, 2024. Extracted 6.16.2024. https://apnews.com

Becker, Sam. *Dartmouth Men's Basketball Team Voted to Unionize. The Timing is Just Right.* March 13, 2024. BBC. Extracted 6.16.2024. www.bbc.com

Deloitte Development LLC. *Dbriefs: Activating New Department of Labor Fair Labor Standards Act Changes.* March 6, 2024. www2.deloitte.com

Department of Labor. *The Fair Labor Standards Act (FLSA).* Extracted 6.17.2024. www.dol.gov

Department of Labor. *Individual Coverage.* Extracted 6.21.2024. www.dol.gov

Internal Revenue Service. *Full-Time Student.* Extracted 6.21.2024. www.irs.gov

Internal Revenue Service. *Independent Contractor Defined.* Updated August 2, 2023. Extracted 6.16.2024. www.irs.gov

National Archives. *National Labor Relations Act (1935).* Extracted 6.17.2024. www.archives.gov

National Labor Relations Board. *Case: University of Southern California; Pac-12 Conference; National Collegiate Athletics Association.* Filed February 8, 2022. Case files available at: www.nlrb.gov/case/31-CA-290326

National Labor Relations Board. *Northwestern University and College Athletes Players Association (CAPA), Petitioner.* August 17, 2015. Decision on Review and Order. Extracted 6.16.2024. www.nlrb.gov

Chapter 10

Camillo, Lynne A. *Office of Chief Counsel Memorandum: Whether Operation of an NIL Collective Furthers an Exempt Purpose Under Section 501(c)(3).* Released June 9, 2023. Internal Revenue Service. Extracted 6.03.2024. www.irs.gov

Internal Revenue Service. *Exempt Organizations Technical Guide: TG 48: Unrelated Business Income Tax.* Revision date 12/15/2023. Extracted 4.14.2024. www.irs.gov

Internal Revenue Service. *Revenue Ruling 80-296, 1980-2 C.B. 195.* Extracted 5.05.2024. www.irs.gov

Merriam Webster Dictionary. *Education.* www.merriam-webster.com

Chapter 11

Connor, Bran. *College Sports Proves Integral to Olympic Movement.* July 23, 2021. National Collegiate Athletic Association. Extracted 7.14.2024. www.ncaa.org

Gough, Christina. *Count of Active NFL Players in 2024 by Country.* March 12, 2024. Statista. Extracted 7.13.2024. www.statista.com

Gough, Christina. *MLB Players on Opening Day Rosters 2013-2024.* June 24, 2024. Statista. Extracted 7.13.2024. www.statista.com

Gough, Christina. *Total Revenue of Major League Baseball Teams 2023.* January 2, 2025. Statista. Extracted 1.05.2025. www.statista.com

Gough, Christina. *Total Revenue of the National Basketball Association 2001-2024.* October 25, 2024. Statista. Extracted 1.05.2025. www.statista.com

Gough, Christina. *Total Revenue of the National Hockey League 2005-2023.* April 23, 2024. Statista. Extracted 7.12.2024. www.statista.com

Gough, Christina. *Total Revenue of the NFL 2001-2023.* October 1, 2024. Statista. Extracted 1.05.2025. www.statista.com

Infoplease. *Total Players in the NFL.* Updated July 24, 2020. Extracted 7.13.2024. www.infoplease.com

Kerr, Emma and Wood, Sarah. *See the Average College Tuition in 2023-2024.* September 20, 2023. U.S. News & World Report. Extracted 6.30.2024. www.usnews.com

Knight-Newhouse College Athletics Database. *Football Bowl Subdivision (FBS): Where the Money Comes From.* 2023. Knight Commission on Intercollegiate Athletics and Syracuse University Newhouse School of Public Communications. Extracted 6.29.2024. https://knightnewnousedata.org

Loughead, Katherine. *State Corporate Income Tax Rates and Brackets, 2024.* January 23, 2024. Tax Foundation. Extracted 10.23.2024. https://taxfoundation.org

National Basketball Association G League Tracker. *G League Contracts/Finances.* Extracted 6.30.2024. https//gleague.nba.com

Rudell, BJ. *How Much Do XFL Players Make? Breaking Down Salaries After the Season's End.* May 13, 2023. Pro Football Network. Extracted 6.30.2024. www.profootballnewtork.com

Statista Research Department. *NBA Number of Players Used Each Season 2011-2022.* September 7, 2023. StatistaExtracted 7.13.2024. www.statista.com

Chapter 12

Bissinger, Buzz. *Why College Football Should be Banned*. Updated May 8, 2012. The Wall Street Journal. Extracted 7.22.2024. www.wsj.com

Britannica. *Sports and Recreation*. Extracted 7.16.2024. www.britannica.com

DiSalvo, David. *Is Malcolm Gladwell Right, Should College Football Be Banned to Save Brains?* Updated July 22,2013. Forbes. Extracted 7.23.2024. www.forbes.com

ESPN. *UC Riverside Won't Cut Sports, will Compete at Division I Level Despite Pandemic*. Extracted 7.28.2024. www.espn.com

Fry, John A. *We're Glad to Say No to College Football*. January 3, 2016. The Wall Street Journal. Extracted 1.05.2025. www.wsj.com

Gauthier, Brendan. *Football Returns, Unofficially*. October 1, 2010. BU Today. Extracted 7.28.2024. www.bu.edu

Grasgreen, Allie. *Beyond Sports: Spelman is Eliminating Intercollegiate Athletics and Withdrawing from NCAA Competition, Instead Focusing on a Campus-Wide Wellness Initiative that Emphasizes Fitness for Everyone*. October 31, 2012. Inside Higher Education. Extracted 7.22.2024. www.insidehighered.com

Iona University Athletics. *Iona Will No Longer Sponsor Football*. Extracted 7.28.2024. https://ionageals.com

Jatoi, Sajad. *Sports Amid Chaos in Afghanistan*. September 29, 2021. The Diplomat. Extracted 7.28.2024. https://thediplomat.com

Mertes, Michah. *The Fall of Creighton Football*. November 9, 2021. Crieghton University. www.creighton.edu

Morse, Ben. *Student Government Pushes to Revive Football at American* University. May 29, 2022. The Eagle. Extracted 7.28.2024. https://theeagle.com

Most, Doug. *50 Years Ago, the BU Football Team Played Its Only Bowl Game.* December 5, 2019. Bostonia. Extracted 1.05.2025. www.bu.edu

Neiburg, Jeff. *Would John Fry Try to Kill Temple Football? He Wrote an Op-Ed that May Offer Some Hints*. Published June 28, 2024; updated July 2, 2024. The Philadelphia Inquirer. Extracted 7.28.2024. www.inquirer.com

Potas, Dace. *Gen Z Doesn't Care About Sports. That's Part of a Bigger Problem*. USA Today. Extracted 1.07.2024. www.usatoday.com

Recchie, Benjamin. *The Chicago Way of Football: There's More to Winning Than You Might Think*. 2019. The Core: College Magazine of the University of Chicago. Extracted 7.28.2024. https://thecore.uchicago.edu

SportEdge. *College Sports in Countries Other than the U.S.* Extracted 7.28.2024

The New York Times. *A GREAT BEQUEST LEAVES COLLEGE IN A QUANDARY; By Provisions of the Will of Anna T. Jeanes Swarthmore Falls Heir to Millions...* October 6, 1907. Extracted 7.17.2024. www.nytimes.com

Walkenhorst, Emily and Boutwell, Christian. *Panel Says No to Start Football at UALR*. February 7, 2019. Arkansas Democrat Gazette. Extracted 7.28.2024. www.arkansasonline.com

Wikipedia. *List of Defunct College Football Teams*. Extracted 7.21.2024. www.wikipedia.com

Chapter 13

Berkowitz, Steve. *NCAA Recorded Nearly $1.3 Billion in Revenue in 2023, Putting Net Assets at $565 Million*. February 1, 2024. USA Today. Extracted 8.18.2024. www.usatoday.com

Bomboy, Scott. *On This Day, Supreme Court Upholds Baseball's Antitrust Exemption*. November 9, 2023. National Constitution Center. Extracted 8.11.2024. https://constitutioncenter.org

Chapman, Michelle and Koenig, David. *JetBlue and Spirit are Ending Their $3.8 billion Merger Plan After a Federal Judge Blocked the Deal*. Updated March 4, 2024. Associated Press. Extracted 8.06.2024. https://apnews.com

ESPN. *Congressmen Propose Bill that Would Protect the NCAA*. Extracted 8.18.2024. www.espn.com

Federal Election Commission. *Mission and History*. Extracted 8.18.2024. www.fec.gov

Federal Railroad Administration. *About FRA*. Extracted 1.01.2025. https://railroads.dot.gov

Federal Trade Commission. *Clayton Act*. Extracted 8.06.2024. www.ftc.gov

Fox Sports. *US Court Rules Some NCAA Athletes May Qualify as Employees Under Federal Wage-and-Hour Laws*. July 11, 2024. Extracted 8.18.2024. www.foxsports.com

Gwartney, James D. and Sobel, Richard L. *Economics: Private and Public Choice.* Ninth Edition. 2000. The Dryden Press: A Division of Harcourt College Publishers. Pg. 908

Lupion, Adam M., Fox, Joshua S. and Gobel, David R. of Proskauer Rose LLP – Labor Relations Update. *House Considers Bill Declaring Student Athletes Not Employees.* June 15, 2024. Extracted 8.18.2024. https://natlawreview.com

North Carolina Utilities Commission. *About the NC Utilities Commission.* February 2024 Commission Informational Review. Extracted 8.11.2024.

Surface Transportation Board. *About STB.* Extracted 1.01.2025. www.stb.gov

U.S. National Archives & Records Administration. *Sherman Antitrust Act (1890).* Extracted 8.06.2024. www.archives.gov

United States Congress. *S.53 – Curt Flood Act of 1998.* October 27, 1998. Extracted 8.11.2024. www.congress.gov

List of Abbreviations

ABC	American Broadcasting Company
ACC	Atlantic Coast Conference
AOA	American Olympic Association (later the USOA, USOC and USOPC)
BCS	Bowl Championship Series (started 1998; discontinued in 2013)
CBS	Columbia Broadcasting System
CFA	College Football Association (catalyzed the landmark anti-trust lawsuit against the NCAA in the 1970s and 1980s)
CFP	College Football Playoff
DOJ	Department of Justice
DOL	Department of Labor
FBS	Football Bowl Subdivision (formerly Division 1-A)
FCS	Football Championship Subdivision (formerly Division 1-AA)
FLSA	Fair Labor Standards Act
GAAP	Generally Accepted Accounting Principles
IAUS	Intercollegiate Athletic Association of the United States (the precursor to the NCAA)
IFRS	International Financial Reporting Standards
IOC	International Olympic Committee
IRC	Internal Revenue Code (can refer to any of the three main codifications —1939, 1954, 1986—as well as the current one as written today)
IRS	Internal Revenue Service
MAAC	Metro Atlantic Athletic Conference
NAIA	National Association of Intercollegiate Athletics (a competitor to the NCAA)
NBA	National Basketball Association
NBC	National Broadcasting Company
NCAA	National Collegiate Athletic Association
NFL	National Football League
NGB	National Governing Body (governs certain Olympic sports in a given country)
NIL	Name, Image and Likeness
NIT	National Invitational Tournament
NLRA	National Labor Relations Act (created the NLRB)
NLRB	National Labor Relations Board
NOL	Net Operating Loss

NOLI	National Letter of Intent
OBS	Olympic Broadcasting Services
PCC	Pacific Coast Conference (later the Pacific 8, PAC-10 and PAC-12)
PGA	Professional Golf Association
SEC	Southeastern Conference
TRA	Tax Reform Act of 1976
UBTI	Unrelated Business Taxable Income
USGA	United States Golf Association
USOA	United States Olympic Association (later the USOC and USOPC)
USOC	United States Olympic Committee (later the USOPC)
USOPC	United States Olympic & Paralympic Committee
USTA	United States Tennis Association

www.ingramcontent.com/pod-product-compliance
Lightning Source LLC
Chambersburg PA
CBHW031530120626
46545CB00005B/2081